PENGUIN BUSINESS
THE MONEY BALL

An investment banker with over a decade of experience in start-up advisory, Sarthak Ahuja is a gold medallist from the Indian School of Business (ISB) and the bestselling author of *Daily Coffee and Startup Fundraising* and *Founder's Office*.

Having been the youngest Indian with four degrees—in CA, CS, CMA and a bachelor's degree in finance—all by the age of twenty-three, he started his career as a chartered accountant in the areas of corporate finance, valuations and transaction advisory. He currently works as an executive coach with select founders, helping them scale their business to international markets, and is known by the masses for his daily videos on social media on the subjects of finance, business development and real estate.

A faculty member for finance at institutes such as ISB and the face of CNBC TV18's show *Behind the Billions*, you can join his three-million strong community on Instagram (@casarthakahuja), LinkedIn and YouTube.

THE
MONEY BALL

YOUR GUIDE TO CRAFTING
BUSINESS IDEAS AND FUNDRAISING

SARTHAK **AHUJA**

PENGUIN
BUSINESS

An imprint of Penguin Random House

PENGUIN BUSINESS

Penguin Business is an imprint of the Penguin Random House group of companies whose addresses can be found at global.penguinrandomhouse.com

Published by Penguin Random House India Pvt. Ltd
4th Floor, Capital Tower 1, MG Road,
Gurugram 122 002, Haryana, India

First published in Penguin Business by Penguin Random House India 2025

Copyright © Sarthak Ahuja 2025

All rights reserved

10 9 8 7 6 5 4 3 2

The views and opinions expressed in this book are the author's own and the facts are as reported by him which have been verified to the extent possible, and the publishers are not in any way liable for the same.

Please note that no part of this book may be used or reproduced in any manner for the purpose of training artificial intelligence technologies or systems.

ISBN 9780143473237

Typeset in Adobe Garamond Pro by MAP Systems, Bengaluru, India
Printed at Thomson Press India Private Limited

This book is sold subject to the condition that it shall not, by way of trade or otherwise, be lent, resold, hired out or otherwise circulated without the publisher's prior consent in any form of binding or cover other than that in which it is published and without a similar condition including this condition being imposed on the subsequent purchaser.

www.penguin.co.in

Contents

Introduction	vii
Section One: Are You Ready to Be an Entrepreneur—Before You Get Started	1
Section Two: Spotting Business Opportunities	19
Section Three: Business Planning and Set-Up	59
Section Four: Funding Fundamentals	81
Section Five: Funding Brass Tacks	139
Section Six: Getting the Deal Through	213
Section Seven: Basics of Business Compliance That a Founder Must Know	244
Afterword	257
Acknowledgements	259

Introduction

There could be many reasons why you decided to pick up this book. Perhaps a compelling idea is keeping you awake at night and you are itching to execute it. It could also well be that you are keen to grow your family business, professionalize operations and/or diversify offerings. In the many interactions that I have had with people who are keen to start up, the overwhelming reason, however, has always been that they crave independence and wish to work for themselves on their own terms. Large-scale, institutionalized data seems to suggest the same trend:

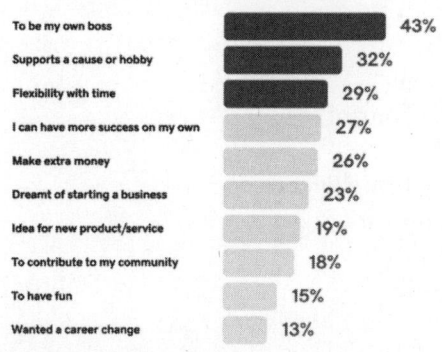

Whatever may be your reason to take this path, the truth is that entrepreneurship is not for the faint of heart. Neither can any formal degree fully prepare you for the real-world challenges of navigating uncharted waters. In my journey as an investor and educator, I have worked with close to a hundred start-ups, advising them across financial, legal, fundraising as well as business aspects. Through this process, I have seen a multitude of founder challenges, up close. Overall, I have come to realize that founders are built less by education and more by character. You must have the grit, resilience and constant enthusiasm and curiosity to innovate and build something new. Entrepreneurship is a lot about combining what you know with a willingness to adapt, learn on the fly, fail and rise again.

Little surprise then that in taking bets on businesses, investors are known to evaluate the idea as much as the people executing it. I have often quoted an interesting framework developed by Matrix Partners that evaluates entrepreneurs on whether or not they have the traits required to navigate the ups and downs that are par for the course in entrepreneurship. The nine aspects that they have listed include:

1. Curiosity
2. Grit
3. Hunger
4. Self-Control
5. Zest
6. Social Intelligence
7. Optimism
8. Gratitude
9. Hustle

If I had to add another trait to this list, it would be learning agility. We live in a VUCA (volatile, uncertain, complex, ambiguous) world where the ability to learn and adapt to changing circumstances is a key life skill.

The framework above requires you to evaluate yourself on the nine parameters, giving yourself a score of 0, 0.5 or 1 on each. As a thumb rule, a total score above 6 is considered encouraging and is telling of your likely success as an entrepreneur.

All of this is good, I hear you say. The bigger concern that you may have is how to choose that winning idea that can make your entrepreneurial project fly. Well, by now we have all heard that successful start-ups exist because they solve a large enough problem. A start-up idea, in other words, is about offering a unique or disruptive solution to a problem experienced by a large number of people. How do you ascertain, though, that your idea is unique and disruptive? I quite like the Delta 4 principle that Kunal Shah, the founder of Cred and Freecharge, has postulated that helps you evaluate revolutionary ideas. Let's take an example to understand it. Remember the days you had to stand in long, serpentine queues to pay convenience bills . . . electricity, water or others? Odds are you may not have done it yourself but your parents can vouch for the time and effort it took to do so. Compare that with pulling out your phone with a flourish now and heading to an app that allows you to pay these bills within seconds. Now, go ahead and rate the previous experience and the current one on a scale of 1 to 10, where 1 is poor and 10 is outstanding. Odds are that you would rate the previous experience as 1 and the current one as 9. What you need to do next is calculate the difference between the two—in this case, 8. The Delta 4 principle states that for any idea to be potentially revolutionary, this delta or difference should be 4 or higher. Go ahead and apply this principle to other examples that you can think of and sure enough, you will see the theory working in each case. Now, here's the critical part: What if you applied this theory to your start-up idea? Is the delta 4 or higher?

As you go ahead and read the chapters to come, we will discuss several aspects that will enable you to start and navigate your entrepreneurial journey. Needless to say, embarking on this journey is an exhilarating yet daunting adventure. This book is crafted with a singular purpose: to simplify the process for you. From the spark of an innovative idea to securing that crucial round of funding, my hope is to offer practical insights and actionable advice every step of the way. Together, let's turn your dream into a thriving reality.

You can also find me on my Instagram handle (@casarthakahuja) where I upload videos to simplify some complex (and not so complex) start-up-related topics daily.

Let's kick-start our journey!

Section One

Are You Ready to Be an Entrepreneur—Before You Get Started

- Mindset: Deferred Gratification, Risk, No Fixed Salary, Social Concerns
- Ikigai Framework: Passion, Opportunity, Skill
- Finances: Bootstrapping, Emergency Funds, Funding Rounds
- Jack of All Trades; Master of One

'Entrepreneurship is living a few years of your life like most people won't, so you can spend the rest of your life like most people can't,' goes a famous quote.

While all of us aspire towards the life that the latter half of the quote hints at, the journey needs to begin by assessing if we are indeed ready for the first half. That is exactly where we need to begin—by looking at some of the prerequisites to take this tough yet life-changing road.

The Entrepreneurial Mindset

We have all heard about how entrepreneurship offers solutions to a wide range of challenges besides sparking innovation and fuelling economies. To do this, there needs to be an important catalyst in place—an entrepreneurial mindset. That resilient, resourceful and solutions-oriented approach that is unshaken even in the most adverse circumstances.

While all of this sounds extremely heroic, even magical, it needs deep reflection for you to ascertain if you indeed have the mindset required to succeed. My suggestion would be to get down to the brass tacks and think of the following four aspects in particular to ascertain your entrepreneurial readiness quotient.

1. Deferred Gratification

You may have heard of the famous marshmallow experiment conducted at Stanford University in the 1960s that explored the benefits of delayed gratification. Essentially, children were seated in a room with a single marshmallow on a plate and were told they could eat it now, or wait fifteen minutes, which would allow them to receive two marshmallows in place of one. The study found that the children who opted to wait tended to have better life outcomes, including but not limited to higher SAT scores, lower BMI, fewer instances of substance abuse and more.

The Marshmallow Test provides powerful lessons that are directly applicable to entrepreneurship. After all, it could take several months or years of hard work before you can start seeing profitability in your business and achieve healthy cash flows. All this while, however, you have to be able to make decisions that set your business up to win in the long-term. In the context of entrepreneurship then, embracing delayed gratification means investing time, effort and resources into building a solid foundation for the business, rather than seeking quick profits. The question to ask yourself is: Are you willing to grind day after day, laying the groundwork for the future. Can you dedicate yourself to business fundamentals even as you delay immediate gratification?

If your answer to the above questions is a well-thought-out yes, odds are that you will be able to create value, foster innovation and achieve lasting success in your venture.

2. Risk

In December 2008, Tesla (that produced high-end electric cars) and SpaceX (that built rockets) were on the verge of financial collapse. The year had been tough for the founder, Elon Musk, since both companies were in trouble and cash was down to nothing. Musk needed $40 million to keep Tesla afloat. He pieced together $20 million of his own money and leaned on investors to match the amount. The nail-biting story of a last-minute rescue that prevented Tesla from bankruptcy and preserved the electric car dream at a time when major US car companies had abandoned electric vehicle production is told in a biography by the acclaimed journalist and writer Walter Isaacson. Entrepreneurial folklore is replete with other such examples of entrepreneurs who took massive risks. In fact, if there is one quality that is common to all entrepreneurs—whether they spearhead an early-stage start-up or are leading a company that clocks hundreds of millions of dollars in revenue—it has to be their ability to take game-changing risks. Simply put, risk-taking is the willingness to take chances in the pursuit of gain, even when the outcome is uncertain. Some of the many risks that entrepreneurs face include leaving a steady pay cheque, using personal savings with no guarantee of a return on investment, misjudging customer interest in a product or service . . . the list goes on. So much so that risk is said to be what's left over after you think you've thought of everything.

When you talk to people about what it means to be a 'risk-taker,' however, most people will begin describing daredevils and gamblers. Yet, that is not what risk-taking in terms of entrepreneurship means. Above anything, successful entrepreneurs need to be calculated risk-takers.

Ask yourself where you score on the 'calculated risk-taking' scale. Do you have a preference for working with certainty and are you paralysed by fear when it comes to decision-making? Or do you thrive on taking measured risks? That said, taking calculated risks is like building a muscle. It's not easy and it takes practice, but done well, you can actually start to enjoy it. Importantly, it is this ability to take calculated risks that, in turn, allows the founders to enjoy a huge upside on account of their high ownership stakes, when the start-up begins to grow.

3. No Fixed Salary

'Dear Customer, Acct XXXX is credited with Rs XXXX on 1 January. Info: Salary'

This is one familiar ping that many of us take delight in on the first of every month. If you are making a transition to entrepreneurship from a corporate role, you particularly need to think this aspect through very carefully, for it is a pleasure that you will have to forgo at least in the early stages. It goes without saying that this comes with several lifestyle and mindset adjustments that you need to be prepared for.

That said, it is also important to state that your ability to negotiate your salary grows as the start-up transitions through various stages. Below are a few benchmarks that are prevalent in the industry and can be used to decide your own salaries at various stages of fundraising, a concept that we will delve into in detail in some of the later chapters:

- **Seed**: Most founder salaries at the seed stage are just enough to manage their basic personal expenses. Salaries at this stage can range between Rs 1 lakh and Rs 1.5 lakh per month, depending on the city you're living in and the amount of funding the start-up has raised. As a thumb rule, no more than 10 per cent of the total funding amount goes into the hands of the founders if the funding is less than Rs 2 crore.
- **Series A**: At this point, you should negotiate with investors to double the salary payout to a monthly in-hand amount, which is at par with the talent the start-up has to hire on closing Series A.
- **Series B**: It is best to negotiate a secondary sale of some shareholding to incoming investors so as to generate some cash in hand, which can be used for building assets and savings. This is the first opportunity for the founder to cash out on their work and effort.

These are, of course, just indicative estimates. Actual salaries and founder payouts may vary with industry, size of the fundraise and need of the business.

4. Social Concerns

My wife comes from a family of people employed in top corporates. She herself was happily employed with Meta before taking the leap of faith to join me in my entrepreneurial venture. Needless to say, in the early stages she was hesitant to take the road less travelled. Understandably so, for it is not easy to let go of a job with defined responsibilities, fixed salary and defined reporting structures, in order to venture into uncharted terrain.

To add to your predicament, you are also faced with a host of social concerns. Friends and family could be calling you out on your decision to leave a cushy job, terming it untenable. Besides, you could also be witnessing the seemingly perfect lives of your peers on social media, replete with fancy vacations. It is the willingness to forgo social validation and deal with tons of ambiguity that is a big perquisite to the entrepreneurial path.

On the other extreme, if you are headed to the world of entrepreneurship driven by the glitz and glamour of newspaper headlines—of large funding rounds and the making of unicorns—you need to remember that behind every such headline are many more stories of pain and struggle that entrepreneurs need to be mentally prepared for. Think of any entrepreneur you look up to and odds are they have had more than their share of struggles and failure. Before Amazon became the huge success that it is today, Jeff Bezos had an array of failed ideas. Before starting PayPal and investing in companies like Facebook, Peter Thiel's early hedge fund, Clarium Capital, reportedly lost 90 per cent of its $7 billion assets on the stock market, currencies and oil prices. Closer home, similar stories abound where entrepreneurs who are now seen as being extremely successful had to overcome the failure of several start-ups. Let these examples serve as encouragement to learn from your mistakes and remain steadfast on your path.

Ikigai Framework: Passion, Opportunity, Skill, Willingness to Pay

Having undertaken a brief assessment of your mindset and whether or not it is conducive to the rocky yet hugely fulfilling road to entrepreneurship, it is time now to move to the next important aspect—namely, how do you zero down on an effective idea?

There are several frameworks that help evaluate the feasibility of a business idea that are largely based on whether or not the idea solves a large enough problem, creates an impact and makes you some wealth in the bargain. While we will speak of spotting business opportunities in detail in a later section, I would like to introduce a framework that I find particularly helpful.

The POS framework has three important constituents:

- **Passion**
- **Opportunity**
- **Skill Set**

In choosing an idea, you need to carefully evaluate three factors: whether you are passionate about the idea, if there is a market opportunity for it and whether or not you have complementary skills to see the idea to fruition. It stands to reason that if you have the passion for something and there's a huge market opportunity for it but you do not have complementary skills to execute it, you are likely to fail. On the other hand, if there is an opportunity in the market for which you have the necessary skill set but no passion, you might make some money but with drudgery. After all, how long can you keep working on something you are not passionate about? Eventually, you will be exhausted. Conversely, if you have the passion and the requisite skills but there isn't a large enough market opportunity, you may enjoy the experience but receive limited returns on your investment and eventually give up. All three: Passion, Opportunity and Skill Set, therefore need to be aligned for the business to work.

The POS framework, in turn, seems to have been inspired by the concept of *Ikigai*.

What Is Ikigai?

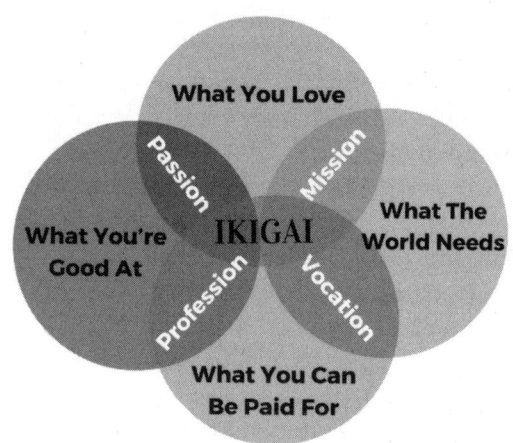

Ikigai is a Japanese concept that helps us identify our core purpose of living. The word ikigai is a combination of two words: *iki*, which means 'to live' and *gai*, which means 'reason'. Simply put, therefore, ikigai means 'reason for being'.

Finding your ikigai involves discovering the sweet spot where four essential elements meet: what you love, what you are good at, what the world needs and what you can be paid for. In the context of entrepreneurship, ikigai can serve as a powerful framework to guide your journey and ensure that your business endeavours are both fulfilling and impactful.

While we deep dive into the four elements, I also urge you to undertake a short exercise that can help you arrive at your own ikigai.

What You Love

It goes without saying that you need to begin by choosing a problem that you are passionate about solving. Among other things, it is this passion towards the cause that will ensure you stay true to the course when things become tough.

To do that, take some time to list down activities and interests that you love. Think about causes that get you all fired up. It will also help you to reflect on moments that make you feel alive and fulfilled.

Let us for a moment assume that in doing this exercise you discover your passion for creating stylish clothing that minimizes environmental impact. Let us park this finding aside.

What You Are Good At

Having passion is great, but enthusiasm alone can get you only so far. In order to make a real difference, what you also need to have is the right expertise that allows you to execute your passion.

At this stage, it will help to list down what you think are your core competencies. That done, map them with your passion to arrive at potential areas where you can offer workable solutions.

To follow the above example through, if your core competencies reveal that you have the technical expertise to create high-quality clothing, you could be on to something as it matches your passion.

What the World Needs

Being passionate about a problem and having the right skills is one part of the equation; an important one at that. However, you also need to figure out if the problem that you are setting out to solve is indeed a big problem for people. Remember the Delta 4 principle I referred to earlier? In short, you need to determine if your solution will really make a tangible difference in the lives of people.

In the above example, it is a definite plus that the world needs more sustainable practices in the fashion industry to reduce waste, pollution and the exploitation of resources.

What You Can Be Paid For

Well, all of the above done, if the solution that you have on offer isn't something that people are likely to pay you for, it can at best be referred to as a hobby and not a business. Focusing on solutions that can be monetized is therefore key.

In the example above, with a growing market demand for sustainable and ethical fashion, you could well be on your way to finding your ikigai.

While we have delved on the concept of ikigai in some detail, what is ironic, however, is that, on ground, we barely focus on the four factors. In fact, the way we actually choose our careers is by pursuing degrees that may be in demand and that could help us find quick employment. This pathway can be severely limiting. As renowned entrepreneur and investor Naval Ravikant suggests, if you need a degree to do a job, your earning potential is likely to be limited.

Finding your ikigai is not a moment when the circles in a Venn diagram converge and you know what you need to do for the rest of your life.

It's discovered through constant action—almost like foraging for it in a forest. You start on one path, but over the course, keep taking turns and detours along the way, when what you have been looking for suddenly yet slowly appears.

And when you do find it, you need to go all in, which may also mean needing capital or funds to execute it with all your might.

It's fair to not have capital on your own. The beauty of the world economy today is such that you can take such bets on your passion and purpose while accessing capital available from several channels.

As a next step, we would want to understand how to find and navigate through the ways of securing capital.

Finances

An extremely important aspect to figure out before you set out on your entrepreneurial journey is, no marks for guessing: finances. A cornerstone of entrepreneurship, finances play a pivotal role in every stage of a business's lifecycle. If, for instance, you began your start-up as a side hustle, you will soon notice that its demands begin to increase. At this time, the founders typically put in their own money largely by way of their salaries or past savings. This is what is popularly known as bootstrapping the business and the source of funds is referred to as 'Founder's Funds'. Running a business also necessitates setting up an emergency fund or a contingency fund to take care of business uncertainty and keep the company afloat.

Most people, though, are financially limited in their individual capacity. If the business revolves around a tangible product to be sold, working capital challenges arise. If it's a tech product, you'd be constrained to hire the right people to build it out. At this point, it becomes crucial to consider external funding, the overarching purpose of which is almost always survival or growth.

In the subsequent section, let's understand the different sources of external funds and the characteristics of these investors.

Family and Friends

Typically, your first source to turn to for funding is likely to be financing by friends and family. This can either take the form of debt-funding or an equity transaction where these investors are formally allotted shares of your start-up. Usually, founders are known to take the former route as it's easier to execute, especially since borrowing money from friends and family does not typically come with the pressure of any interest to be paid. This debt is usually of a convertible nature that later converts to equity. We will discuss the concept of a convertible note in some detail later in the book.

Among other things, it is your job to evaluate whether the funds you have raised from your friends and family in the first round are enough to sustain you until you raise the first external round or until the business becomes self-sustaining. You should have a reasonable idea under what circumstances you may need to raise another round of investment from friends and family, what the amount would be and how that will be used. If you do not raise a sufficiently large amount during the early stages of your start-up, you are likely to fall short of finances to grow your business to scale. Shortage of resources, for instance, could lead to a marketing struggle and your target users may never discover your product. Your family and friends too should have prior knowledge of these possibilities, so they can be prepared to put in more money when the need arises. If they do not have that capability to fund you sufficiently again, you'll need to prepare accordingly and plan your progress around it.

A word of caution here: money can be a sensitive topic in India, especially when it comes to friends and family. It's imperative that your family and friends understand the business risks when they invest. Be transparent and clear about how you plan to use the funds and what outcomes you expect to achieve. Nobody wants their money to go towards frivolous ideas or expenses. Additionally, family and friends should be on the same page as far as the vision of the company goes.

Angel Investors

Funding from friends and family can take you only that far. The need for more resources would typically lead you to angel investors. This is the time you raise what is referred to as a seed round to secure a substantial amount to hit the next business milestone. The objective of the seed capital is typically to help you market your product and acquire the first large set of users.

It will be worthwhile to understand who these angel investors typically are. Traditionally, angel investors are high-net-worth individuals (HNIs) who have large personal wealth and investments across asset classes. Their objective, of course, is to optimize their investments while supporting something that they believe in. Since start-ups are a risky asset class, they usually constitute only a small portion of all the angel's total investments towards it. In order to de-risk their portfolio, angel investors invest in a host of start-ups that they find promising. Statistically, many of these start-ups fail and the money invested goes to dust. The upside for the angel investor, however, is that the ones that succeed, often end up not only compensating for the losses made but deliver a decent return (>2x for successful investors) on the total capital invested.

Anupam Mittal of People Group, for instance, has publicly spoken about several companies in his portfolio being shut down without giving any returns. A small number of companies that he invested in, however, helped him not just recover those losses but offer him much greater returns. 'This is called the portfolio approach of investing and you cannot obsess about individual losses,' he was quoted as saying.*

Accelerators

Y Combinator, 500 Start-ups, Sequoia's Surge, Accel Atoms, Techstars.

Odds are that you have heard the above names. All of these are sought-after accelerators that offer founders of early-stage start-ups access to angels and venture capital (VC) networks, professional guidance and investments. Typically, accelerators have the following aspects on offer:

1. **Funding**: Accelerators often provide seed funding in exchange for equity in the start-up.
2. **Mentorship**: Start-ups receive guidance from experienced entrepreneurs, industry experts and investors.
3. **Networking**: They provide access to a network of potential partners, customers and investors.
4. **Education**: Workshops, seminars and training sessions are conducted to help start-ups develop their business skills.
5. **Office Space**: Some accelerators offer physical office space for start-ups to work and collaborate.

Once accepted to the accelerator programme, founders go through training classes and sessions to refine their processes.

---

* '"60-70 companies in my portfolio have shut down without giving any returns:" Anupam Mittal on Shark Tank India 2', BT Upstart, 20 January 2023, https://www.businesstoday.in/entrepreneurship/story/60-70-companies-in-my-portfolio-have-shut-down-without-giving-any-returns-anupam-mittal-on-shark-tank-india-2-366911-2023-01-20

They are guided in all aspects of the business—business model, customer journey, product development, marketing, hiring, leadership and everything else you could think of—besides being given access to an enviable network of resourceful fellow founders and alumni.

Venture Capital Firms

These are the companies that most entrepreneurs dream about wooing. VC firms are investment companies that provide funding to early-stage, high-potential start-ups and businesses in exchange for equity or ownership stakes. They play a crucial role in the start-up ecosystem by offering not just financial support but also strategic guidance, industry connections and mentorship.

Venture money, however, is typically not long-term money. Their idea is to invest in a company until it reaches a sufficient size so that it can be sold to a corporation or so that the institutional public-equity markets can step in and provide liquidity. In essence, the venture capitalist buys a stake in an entrepreneur's idea, nurtures it for a short period of time and then exits.

Strategic Investors

Unlike VCs, strategic investors don't have any target to exit the start-up and generate returns. In fact, they are more likely to be interested in acquiring these start-ups if they satisfactorily fulfil their objectives. Start-up founders opting for such investments must be aware of these possibilities and be willing to lose control in due course.

Conglomerates such as Reliance Industries, Tata Group and Aditya Birla Group make numerous such investments every year.

We will spend a considerable amount of time on the aspect of fundraising later in the book and look at each of these avenues in more detail by way of their participation in different funding rounds.

Jack of All Trades; Master of One

For long, we have used the term 'Jack of all trades, master of none' as a derogatory phrase, generally implying that someone is spreading themselves too thin. Entrepreneurship, however, requires you to be a versatile Jack of all trades while also being a master of one, that is, having deep expertise in one area that offers a competitive edge.

In the early stages of a start-up, resources are usually limited and the founder(s) must wear multiple hats to get things off the ground. This requires you to park your ego outside the door as you juggle multiple aspects of your business. Speak to any early-stage founder and they will subscribe to the fact that they are both the CEO and the peon in the company.

Some of the key roles that founders often play in the early stages of the start-up include:

1. **Visionary and Strategist**:
    o Setting the direction and long-term goals for the company
    o Identifying opportunities and defining the business model
2. **Product Developer**:
    o Involved in creating and refining the product or service
    o Ensuring the offering meets market needs and stands out from competitors

3. **Marketer and Salesperson:**
   o Promoting the product, building brand awareness and driving customer acquisition
   o Closing deals, negotiating contracts and establishing customer relationships
4. **Financial Manager:**
   o Managing budgets, cash flow and financial planning
   o Securing funding and managing investor relations
5. **Operations and HR Manager:**
   o Overseeing day-to-day operations and ensuring efficiency
   o Hiring, training and managing team members
6. **Customer Support:**
   o Interacting with customers, addressing their concerns and collecting feedback
   o Ensuring customer satisfaction and retention

In order to achieve all of this, being a single founder is limiting. A minimum of two and, at best, three founders, typically work well in achieving business goals and collectively shouldering responsibilities. To this end, founders with different individual strengths are always an advantage. For instance, a healthcare tech solution will benefit from a co-founder who is skilled in the healthcare industry while the other founder(s) should ideally be skilled in marketing so they can help the product reach the right customers. Finding the right co-founder with complementary skills and, most importantly, a shared vision and values is therefore key.

Besides looking for co-founders with complementary skills, it's also important to recognize the value of building a strong team. As the company grows, the ability to hire the right experts and delegate responsibilities is what can give wings to the business.

As Peter Drucker said, 'The best way to predict the future is to create it.' In the following sections, we will focus on how entrepreneurs can create the future that they envisage for themselves, brick by brick.

Section Two

Spotting Business Opportunities

- Painkillers versus Supplements: Identified Wants or Innate Needs
- Arbitrage: Cost, Price, Product
- Looking for White Spaces
- Tracking Consumer Trends
- Organizing the Unorganized
- Sources and Methods of Market Research

As someone who is keen to launch a start-up, odds are that you are continuously on the lookout for business ideas. The good news is that the macro variables are working in your favour. For one, India is the world's fastest growing economy and offers an attractive opportunity to start up.

Which Consumer to Build For?

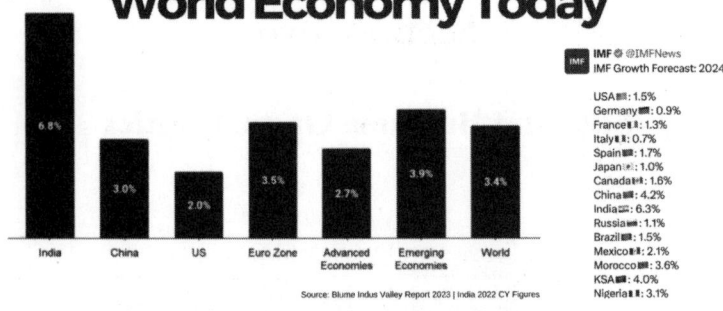

The importance of a large, growing market cannot be emphasized enough. Think of it as a large river on the banks of which massive civilizations thrive, which can support millions of households without showing any signs of distress. Compare and contrast this with a small tributary (read limited market) and you will be able to appreciate the difference. Not only is India's whopping $3.8 trillion economy growing, what works tremendously in its favour is the fact that private consumption drives as much as 60 per cent of India's Gross Domestic Product (GDP); that makes for a whopping $2.22 trillion being spent on private consumption in India. The corresponding numbers for an economy like China, for instance, stand at a low 38 per cent, because a large part of their GDP is from infrastructure-related spending. But that's a conversation for another day. With consumers actively purchasing, start-ups find it easy to validate their business ideas. Importantly, high private consumption allows start-ups to tap into this demand by offering innovative solutions.

If you were to deep dive into the consumer spending habits in India, several other aspects come to light. For one, you will find that Indians spend only 25 per cent of their income on discretionary or non-essential expenses whereas people in China and the US spend a whopping 60 to 70 per cent in the same category.

How much of this are Necessities?

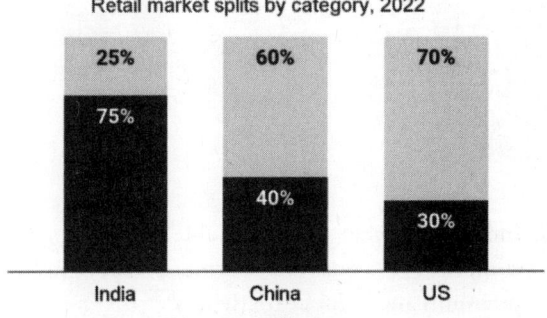

Retail market splits by category, 2022

Source: Blume Indus Valley Report 2024
Macquarie, Bain & Company

For budding entrepreneurs, this may, at first glance, suggest that they should focus on developing products that are in tune with a consumer's essential needs and are in line with their budgetary expectations. That, however, is a rather simplistic way to look at things.

Kishore Biyani, the founder of Future Group, had once said, 'India is a land of many Indias'—a phrase that has been oft-quoted. Nothing can be closer to the truth. The start-up ecosystem lexicon often makes a mention of India's consumer stack comprising India 1, India 2 and India 3. This means classifying Indians into four distinct categories—based on their disposable incomes, consumption habits, and preferences to understand the size of the market that your product or service is aimed to cater to.

Let us look at these unique consumer segments that comprise the Indian market as highlighted by Blume Research.

India 1 'Mexico'	The Consuming Class	~30m households ~120m people ~$15K per person	India1 is the consuming class, and effectively constitutes the market for most startups. Also most startups start here and then expand to India2.	NETFLIX mamaearth CRED NYKAA ZERODHA
India 2 'Indonesia'	The Aspirant Class	~70m households ~300m people ~$3k per person	India2 is the emerging aspirant class. They are heavy consumers and reluctant payers. OTT / media, gaming, edtech and lending are relevant markets for them. UPI and AutoPay has unlocked small ticket spends and transactions from this group.	Jar meesho Kutumb Flipkart STAGE DREAM11 PhonePe
				YouTube MXPLAYER
India 3 'Sub-Saharan Africa'	Unmonetisable Users (& Non-Users)	~205Mn households ~1Bn people ~$1k per person	India3 doesn't have the kind of incomes to be able to spend anything on discretionary goods. They are beyond the pale, as of now, for startups.	Some apps straddle different Indias e.g., Whatsapp, Youtube, Flipkart etc. A good way to understand the above is that all apps in India3 can be used by India2 and India1. Similarly India2 apps can be used by India1. The reverse isn't true. India1 apps are not used by India2 or India3.

- India 1 or what is comparable to the economy of Mexico, comprises a consumer segment that thinks global, shops premium and values experiences.
- India 2 or what is comparable to the Indonesian economy, comprises the aspirant class, which is price-sensitive but brand-loyal and is driven by smart deals.
- India 3 is comparable to the economy of Sub-Saharan Africa, who are the essentials-focused consumers. This group includes the majority of the rural population that is largely unmonetizable.

India is therefore a unique market that is said to contain the economies of Mexico as well as Sub-Saharan Africa in its belly.

But wait, there's more!

India 1, in turn, can be further classified into three sub-segments:

- 1A (Singapore): 5 per cent of India 1—Ultra-luxury, global mindset.
- 1B (Poland): 28 per cent of India 1—Aspirational, balancing quality and affordability.
- 1C (Mexico): 67 per cent of India 1—Brand-curious, thriving in Tier 2/3 cities.

It is India 1, the consuming class that effectively constitutes the market for most start-ups. In fact, if one was to look at the power law in India's consumption, this is how it would pan out for some brands/services:

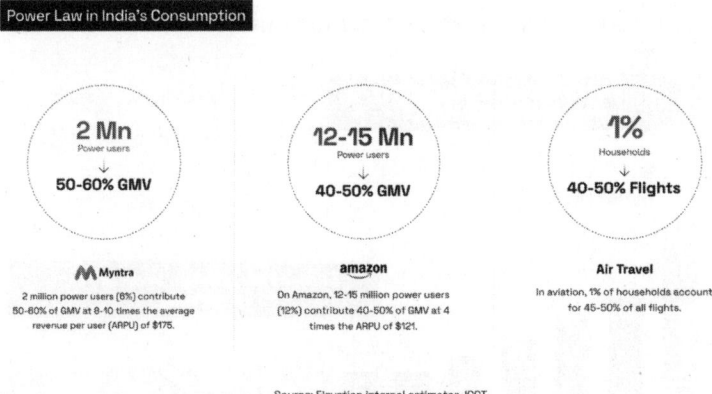

It will also be worth noting here that the rich in India have increased by a whopping 500 per cent over the last decade. This segment, which represents a marginal 2 per cent of India's population, is the one that actually presents an incredible $100 billion opportunity in the next decade.

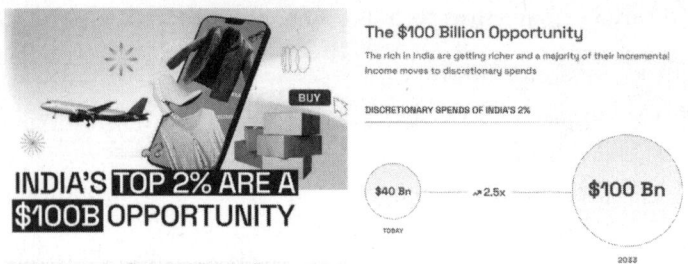

Finally, there is another important group without a mention of which, any conversation on the consumer segments to focus on will not be complete. This comprises the Indian diaspora around the world, which maintains strong ties with the country. This group has about 18 million people with high purchasing power (their annual remittances to India alone make up as much as 3 per cent of India's GDP).

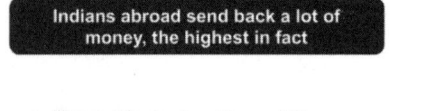

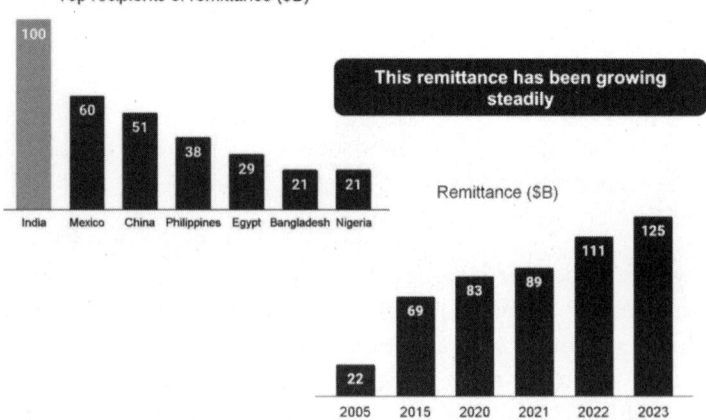

Creative Approaches to Start-up Innovation

The broad consumption canvas laid, let us jump into the task at hand, namely, spotting relevant business opportunities. It will help to begin this discussion with a word of caution. Ever so often, founders get one of the two wrong—the problem or the number of people experiencing it—and only discover their mistakes after months and sometimes years of anguish. It will be worthwhile, therefore, to deep dive into some broad approaches that can help generate effective ideas.

Painkillers versus Supplements

If you look at some of the existing start-ups, you will recognize that they have been able to do either of two things right: identify an unmet demand or cater to a latent need.

Catering to an unmet demand, as the term suggests, implies catering to a market that already exists, albeit with an improved solution. The new solution could add convenience, speed and more. Think of drawing up a grocery list and making your way to the neighbourhood shop to pick up supplies in earlier times. Now, contrast this with quick commerce players delivering groceries (and a lot more) right up to your doorstep in under ten minutes! These players have clearly catered to the unmet need of convenience and paucity of time that plague consumers. There are, in fact, several inspiring stories of entrepreneurs who have catered to unmet needs and, in the process, set up large enterprises. You may have heard the story of Amit Agarwal, an IIT Roorkee alumni, who noticed how sending emails to multiple users that needed to have the same content and yet be personalized for each recipient, was a time-consuming process. This led him to develop niche plug-ins, such as Mail Merge and Document Studio. Today, Mail Merge has over 8 million downloads and Document Studio, over 6 million. His clients include top Fortune 500 companies like LinkedIn, Disney and Uber. Amit is also the founder of

Labnol, an award-winning tech platform/how-to website, and is widely known in tech circles for building key productivity tools that leverage the features of G-Suite, building extremely useful Google add-ons. His is a fascinating story not only of an enterprise that makes over $10 million in revenue each year but importantly of capitalizing the consumer's unmet needs and building a business out of the same.

Catering to a latent need, however, is a bit more complicated since it involves offering solutions to problems that even the consumer isn't quite aware of. For one, it requires deep consumer insights. Think, for instance, of the need of tracking one's basic health indicators—number of steps walked, sleep patterns and more—via a smartwatch. Before smartwatches were launched, the consumer, barring perhaps the most ardent fitness enthusiasts, wouldn't have felt the need themselves to track these health indicators. Yet today, the smartwatch market is projected to reach a market volume of a whopping $40.57 billion by 2029.

While on the subject of customer needs, it will be interesting to see how successful businesses appeal to the fulfilment of customer needs stemming ironically from what has been referred to as the seven deadly sins. Sample this:

7 Sins	Tech Businesses	Traditional Players
Sloth	Urban Company, Zepto	Kirana Home Delivery
Lust	Tinder, OnlyFans, Grindr	Magazines, Content
Gluttony	Zomato, Swiggy, Dominos	Food Businesses
Envy	Instagram	Spy Services
Greed	Myntra, Rummy, Ludo	MLM Companies
Wrath	X (Twitter), Reddit, Angry Birds	TV News Debates
Pride	Superhuman Email	Sneakers, Luxury Apparel

Let us use this traditional seven sins framework as a lens for understanding consumer psychology and market success through a few other examples:

1. Pride (Vanity)
   - Social media platforms like Instagram and TikTok capitalize on people's desire to present an idealized self
   - Luxury brands like Louis Vuitton and Rolex appeal to status-seeking behaviour
   - Premium car manufacturers like Tesla blend status with innovation

2. Greed
   - Investment apps like Robinhood make trading accessible and gamified
   - Cryptocurrency platforms appeal to get-rich-quick aspirations
   - Online gambling sites and mobile games with microtransactions

3. Lust
   - Dating apps like Tinder and Bumble monetize romantic/physical attraction
   - OnlyFans provides a platform for monetizing intimate content
   - Fashion/beauty companies like Victoria's Secret market sensuality

4. Envy
   - LinkedIn capitalizes on professional comparison and status anxiety
   - Review sites like Yelp let people peek into exclusive experiences

- Pinterest creates desire through aspirational lifestyle content

5. Gluttony
    - Food delivery apps like DoorDash/Uber Eats enable instant gratification
    - Streaming services like Netflix encourage binge-watching
    - All-you-can-eat subscription services (food, entertainment, shopping)

6. Wrath
    - Video games with competitive elements/rankings
    - X (formerly Twitter)/Facebook engagement algorithms that promote outrage
    - Review platforms where people can vent frustrations

7. Sloth
    - Food/Groceries delivery services eliminate need to cook/shop
    - Automation products like Roomba reduce physical effort
    - Netflix/streaming services enable passive entertainment

Truly then, being close to the customer can be the source of a wide variety of start-up ideas, as is having a solution-focused mindset.

Arbitrage

What do you have that others don't?

Effectively answering this question can lead you to what is known in economics and finance as an arbitrage opportunity, with the potential to turn into a viable business opportunity.

This could mean something as simple as having a specific talent such as singing or playing an instrument. Cultivated over a period of time, it can help you land gigs and create a strong personal brand. Similarly, based on your expertise, you can create a content page with a strong niche, for example, humour, travel or cooking, and build a subscriber base.

There are also several arbitrage opportunities that already exist in the global markets that can be gainfully leveraged. This involves leveraging factors such as product availability, cost and regulatory and environmental factors. Let us look at some examples to understand these opportunities.

Product Arbitrage

The Government of India has launched a helpful initiative called One District, One Product (ODOP). The ODOP initiative aims to foster balanced regional development by identifying, branding and promoting a unique product from each district in India, to boost local businesses, generate employment and uplift rural economies. What it means for you as an entrepreneur is that it offers you significant opportunities of product arbitrage whereby you can procure the product from the specific district and sell it in a market where it is not readily available.

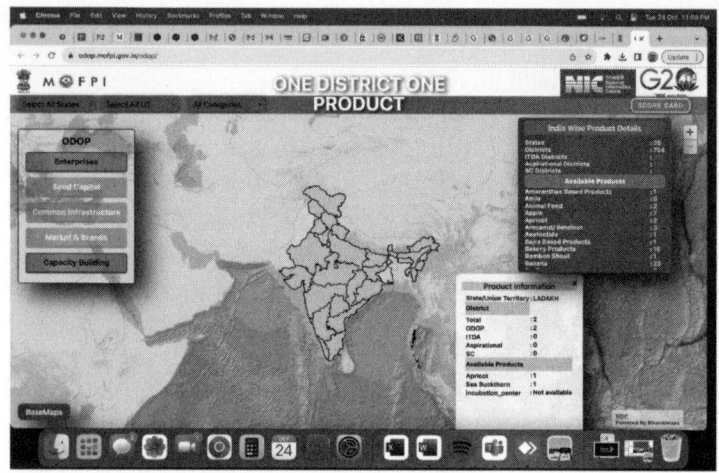

China's import of rice from India is yet another such example. China itself is a major producer of rice, producing close to 30 per cent of the world's rice. However, rice production is a highly water-intensive process that greatly depletes underground water reserves. Producing 1 kg of rice requires nearly 2500 litres of water. Recognizing this factor, China decided to import rice from its neighbour, India and use water and sand instead to build silicon chips that have an increasing global demand. This is a great example of both product arbitrage and better resource management.

Arbitrage is also what is responsible for McKinsey, a service company, being able to break the myth that service companies cannot scale. McKinsey invented the whole concept of a management consultancy, which brought about scientific methodology in how business data is analysed and decisions taken. Over a period of time, it not only analysed data and trends, it also built a valuable database of information and charged other companies for the use of its specialized assets. The company's moat is in its culture and training of the smartest brains as also organizing the knowledge into IP assets that are productized in software solutions and databases. Done successfully, it has led to the company clocking as much as $10+ billion in revenues with a high EBITDA (earnings before interest, taxes, depreciation and amortization).

Cost Arbitrage

Pick up most garments these days and you are sure to find a 'Made in Bangladesh' or 'Made in Vietnam' tag on them—a prime example of a cost arbitrage. When labour or a particular raw material is cheaper in one country as compared to another, you can profit from this cost difference as your cost of production tends to be lower domestically.

This is also what explains the fact that India's software exports reached a whopping $320 billion in 2023. In fact, the services sector contributes significantly to India's growth, accounting for about 55 per cent of the total size of the economy in FY 24.

Price Arbitrage

While cost arbitrage involves leveraging the difference in costs between two markets to maximize profits, price arbitrage on the other hand, focuses on the difference in prices of the same assets in different markets. A packet of fox nuts (makhana) in India, for instance, costs roughly Rs 140 per 100 gm, whereas it can cost upwards of Rs 2000 per 100 gm in the US. There is price arbitrage at play when one buys fox nuts in India in bulk and, even after accounting for import duty and other taxes, makes a significant profit by selling the same in international markets using e-commerce platforms such as eBay and Amazon.

Price Arbitrage Example

In another example, Buddha rice is a type of black rice that is indigenous to eastern UP. This rice costs approx. Rs 200/kg in India, yet it is priced at $56 per 400 grams, i.e. Rs 11,000 per kg in the US.

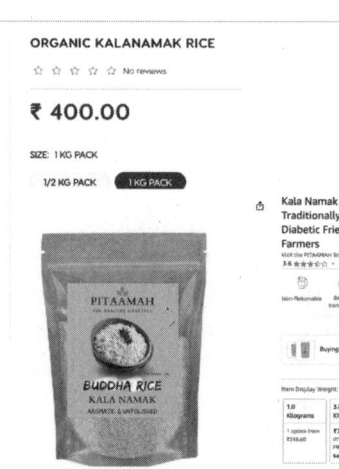

Spotting Business Opportunities

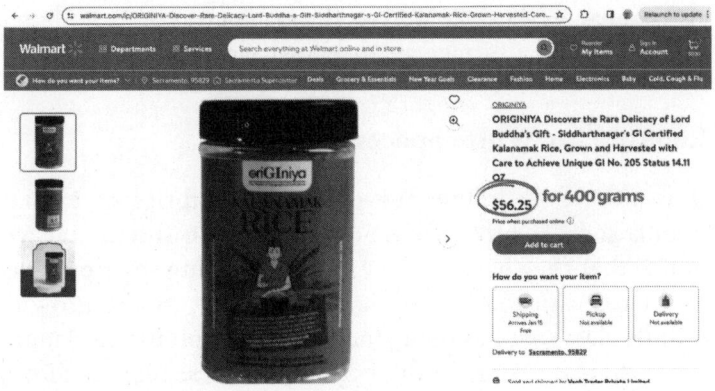

Regulatory Arbitrage

Businesses can also take advantage of differences in regulations in different markets and set up a successful enterprise. Think setting up a crypto business, for instance, where one has to navigate the bureaucracy and regulatory issues of the host nation. Dubai, for instance, offers regulatory arbitrage for crypto companies, as regulations here are more conducive as compared to the US and Europe. Rwanda similarly offers yet another example of regulatory arbitrage for companies involved in drone manufacturing. Similarly, corporations may set up subsidiaries in countries with lower tax rates to minimize their overall tax burden.

Environmental Arbitrage

Ever wondered why Iceland, in the recent past, has become a major hub for crypto mining? The answer, in part, lies in its cold climate. Besides being cost-prohibitive as it involves a great deal of hardware and electricity costs, crypto mining also generates a great deal of heat. There you go, that is environmental arbitrage at work for Iceland!

Looking for White Spaces

If you were to follow the growth trajectories of fashion brands such as H&M, Zara and Uniqlo in India, you will notice that they have actively been expanding their presence in Tier 2 cities across India, capitalizing on the growing middle class that has rising incomes and aspirations. Among other things, a surge in digital usage in these regions during the Covid-19 pandemic enabled consumers to discover and experiment with new brands. Retailers are now looking to tap into this opportunity. What brands such as these are effectively doing is selling access to aspirers in Tier 2 cities, a clear white space.

Off the Shelves

Brands	FY23	FY22	GROWTH % (FY23)
H&M	2,960	2,115	40
Zara	2,563	1,815	41
Levi's	1,781	1,154	54
Lifestyle	11,810	8,101	46
M&S Reliance	1,845	1,211	52
Uniqlo	624	389	60
Pepe Jeans	560	364	54

India sales in ₹ crore Note: % change over FY22
Source: ROC

If there is another big shift in consumption trends, it is being scripted by Gen Z, the generation born between 1997 and 2012. Ranking high on the splurge:save ratio (they contribute to about 17 per cent of India's total consumption), this digitally native cohort is assuming centre stage in India's consumer markets. Not only is this cohort scaling up Internet use cases, driving monthly or daily active users (popularly referred to as MAU/DAU) growth across app ecosystems, Direct-to-Consumer (D2C) brands are also scaling led by the buying power of Gen Z customers. We will deep dive into this cohort later in our discussion when we analyse different target consumers and their willingness to pay. For now, however, it is important to note that they represent a significant white space for brands.

Yet another way of identifying a white space is to look for new form factors. It can lead you to create innovative products that address specific pain points or enhance user experiences in ways that existing products do not. Take, for instance, the fact that when Apple introduced the iPad, it identified a white space between smartphones and laptops, creating a new category of portable computing devices with a unique form factor. Companies like Fitbit and Apple, similarly, found white space in health and fitness tracking by developing wearable devices that combine convenience with advanced health monitoring features.

We have been witnessing change in form factor in the beauty industry as well, with formats such as a lip balm in a keychain for school supply or a sunscreen stick or a sunscreen spray. By rethinking the design, size and usability of products, you can tap into new market segments and set yourself apart from competitors.

Changing demographics—as in the case of targeting men for luxury skincare or cookware brands as well as capitalizing on occasion-based usage, such as outdoor pollution masks or pre-bathing serums—can be yet other instances that help you identify white spaces and create new market segments.

Tracking Consumer Trends

In today's fast-paced market, staying ahead of consumer trends is crucial for start-up success. By understanding and anticipating what consumers want, start-ups can innovate and create products that meet emerging needs. Monitoring real-time data to gather insights into consumer interests and activities is therefore key. Sample this: carbon-plated running shoes, old-money outfits, shilajit products and Russian manicures have seen 435 per cent, 204 per cent, 132 per cent and 125 per cent growth in demand in the period from 2020 to 2024 based on trending topics in popular community platforms such as Instagram, YouTube and Reddit.

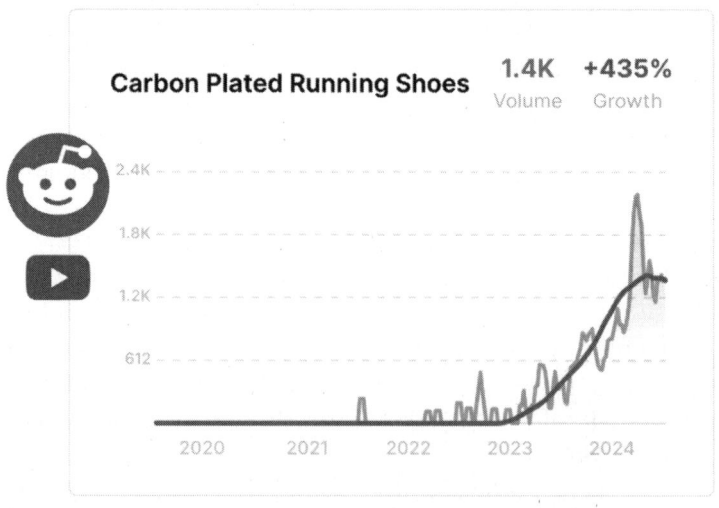

"best carbon plated running shoes"

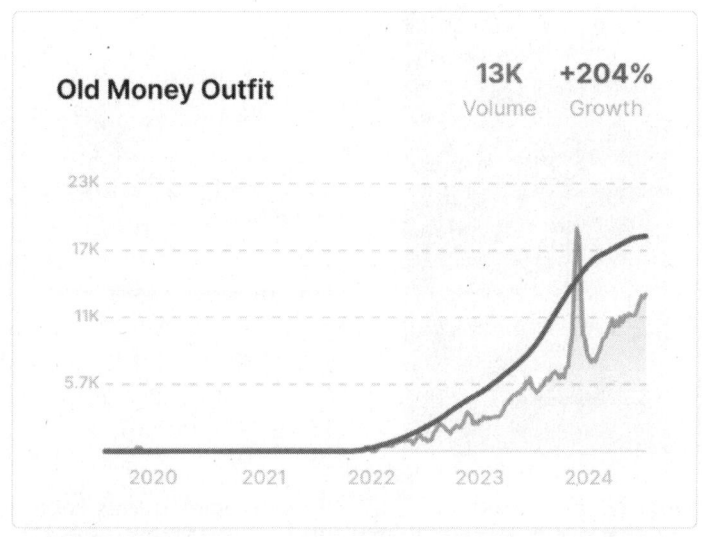

old money outfit **men**

old money outfit **woman**

old money outfit **women**

rasayanam shilajit

shilajit and sea moss

shilajit extract

shilajit vs ashwagandha

shilajit vs sea moss

shilajit vs tongkat ali

upakarma ayurveda pure shilajit

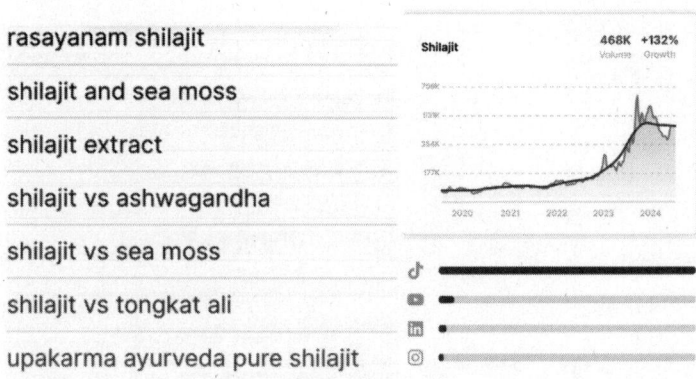

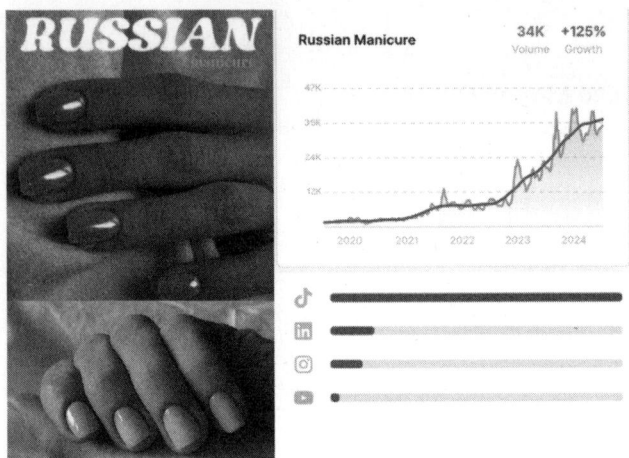

Similarly, new products inspired by societal trends such as pickleball shoes, anti-anxiety jewellery and 3D-printed fashion products are also gaining ground and offer opportunities for budding entrepreneurs.

Importantly, there are several online resources that can help you discover the latest trends and products that are in demand. Some of these include meetglimpse.com, trends.google.com and futurepedia.io (for AI products).

Speaking of emerging trends, trends from other markets take some time to make their way into India and the ensuing information asymmetry can also lead you to interesting business ideas. Think of the popular beauty trend of glass skin that originated in South Korea in recent years or the fact that portable and wearable air purifiers are currently gaining steam in China. Tracking such trends can also lead you to new business ideas.

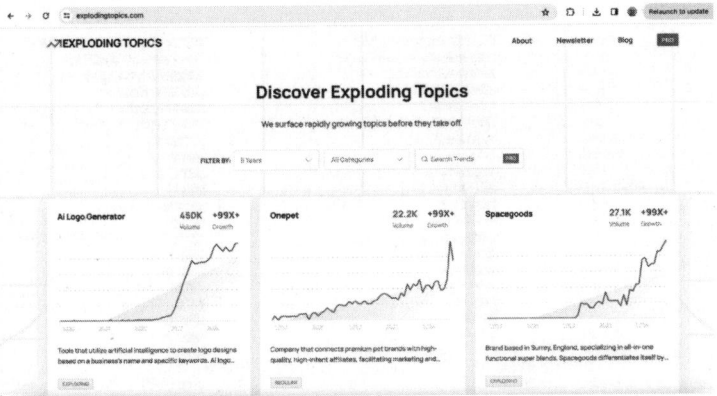

If the idea of a tech start-up excites you and you are interested in uncovering key technological trends in the tech domain, the ABCDE framework can come in handy: A—Artificial Intelligence, B—Biotechnology, C—Crypto and Blockchain, D—Drones and Electronics and E—Energy Transmission.

Leveraging this can help you innovate and gain a competitive edge. AI-powered chatbots improving customer service or using Blockchain in financial services, cloud-based platforms for remote work and more, are all instances of entrepreneurs cashing in on technological advancements.

The consumer app ecosystem in any case has been witnessing rapid growth on the back of the Wang Trifecta—a combination of three key factors: cheap Internet bandwidth, widespread smartphone penetration and a frictionless payment system.

In looking for opportunities, it will be helpful to research and pursue an industry where the growth is at least 1.5x the country's growth, in order to make it a lucrative prospect. As per the 2023 OECD Economic Outlook Report, India demonstrated the highest growth rate (6 per cent), outpacing counterparts such as China.

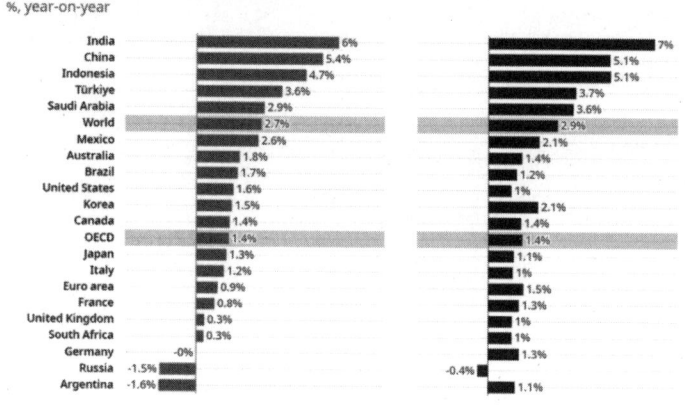

With a 6 per cent base growth rate, you will do well to focus on industries where the growth is at a minimum of 9–10 per cent so you can profit from the differential.

To get you started, below are the most promising industries for the period between 2020 and 2030, as per Invest India. These are industries that have significantly outpaced average growth rates:

Healthcare: 22 per cent p.a.
FMCG and Retail: 12.2 per cent p.a.
Infra and Real Estate: 11.3 per cent p.a.
Finance and Insurance: 15.3 per cent p.a.

Some of the other industries that may be worth your attention, as per the Industry Report on Indian Value Retail Market by Technopak Advisors (March 2024), include home décor, furniture and appliances, food and beverage, media and entertainment, beauty, fashion and personal care, electronics, wearables and robotics. The global beauty market, alone, for instance, rose by 10 per cent in 2023 as seen below.

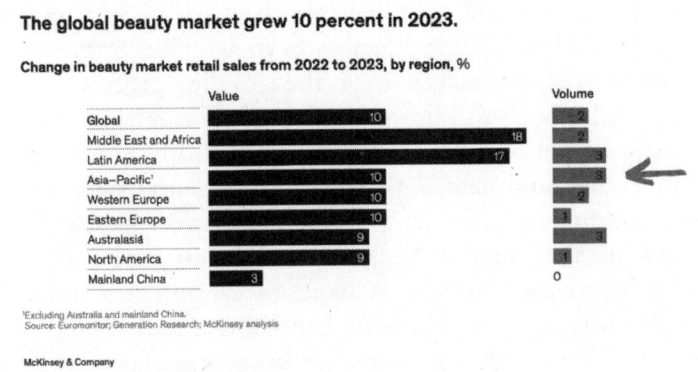

These, of course, are only some initial data points to help you get started on your research. It is important to mention here that while opportunities will continue to evolve over time, what will remain a constant source of advantage is the entrepreneur's skill and ability to spot these opportunities and stay ahead of the curve.

Organizing the Unorganized

Yet another powerful catalyst for start-up ideas is to organize the unorganized. Many successful start-ups have been built on the premise of bringing order to chaos. It could be by way of streamlining processes, bringing about a digital transformation, creating platforms that bring together fragmented markets, undertaking task automation and more.

Let us understand the phenomenon better by way of an example. We all know that multiple scrap collectors or *kabaadiwalas* have existed since time immemorial, across Indian markets. Recykal, an Indian clean-tech start-up, however, took to organizing this unorganized market. They provide digital solutions to connect waste generators (like businesses and consumers) with waste aggregators and recyclers. Their platform facilitates transactions and ensures transparency and traceability in the recycling process.

While Recykal follows a marketplace model, there is a range of other business models to choose from. For instance, you could automate a process that is currently manual, by building a software-as-a-service (SaaS) or enterprise software. You could also take the D2C route to bring order to a fragmented market. A word of caution here though: while entry barriers are low in launching a D2C brand, this model comes with high customer acquisition costs and low brand loyalty.

The choice of the model will to a large extent depend on the moat that you believe you have. Having made a reference to a moat, let us digress a little here to understand what it really is, since this is a term you are likely to hear time and again. A metaphor borrowed from medieval castles, where a moat (a deep, wide ditch filled with water) protected the castle from invaders, a moat is now popularly used to mean a key competitive advantage that sets a company apart from its competitors. Companies can build moats by strengthening their brands, achieving economies of scale or even lobbying for special status from the government. In return, they can receive customer loyalty, pricing power and legal protections that make it difficult for other companies to compete with them.

Below is a clear outline of the different moat possibilities as created by VC veteran, Jerry Neuman.

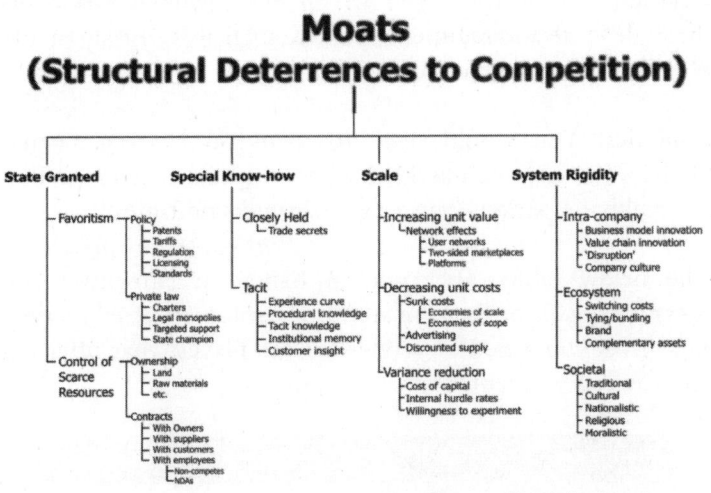

Source: Taxonomy of Moats by Jerry Neumann

Coming back to our topic of organizing the unorganized, let us assume that given the fact that fox nuts are in great demand on account of being regarded as a healthy snack, you want to launch a makhana brand. This would mean having the following aspects in place:

Tech Enabler: You can look at various AI/tech-enabled platforms such as Scale Labs that provide a secure tech infrastructure to enable easy product development and deployment, reducing the need to perform any mundane paperwork or steps.

Marketplace: You will need to ensure that your makhana brand has a strong marketplace presence. It will help that customers are able to purchase your product through frequently visited grocery delivery platforms such as Amazon, Blinkit, etc.

Payments: You will need to enable customer payments through a safe and seamless interface such as Razorpay or any UPI-enabled payment software.

Logistics: You would need to focus on landing a solid logistics partner such as Delhivery, Shiprocket, etc., so that the makhana packets can reach customers on time.

The below table can come in handy in launching and organizing your business in an otherwise unorganized market, as it gives you a good overview of the players that offer the services you will require.

Tech Enabler	Payments	Logistics	Marketplace
Vinculum	Razorpay	Delhivery	amazon
Unicommerce	paytm	Ecom Express	Alibaba Group
KARTROCKET	instamojo	Shiprocket	ebay
zepo	MobiKwik	XPRESSBEES	Etsy
SelluSeller	Cashfree Payments	Shyplite	wish
Shipway	airpay	iThink Logistics	Veepee
primaseller	PhonePe	Shipamax	Cnova
SCALE LABS	BharatPe	Locus	mercado libre
ASSIDUUS	PayGlocal	BLACKBUCK	fruugo

Note: This is not an exhaustive list
Source: Inc42

Inc42

Sources and Methods of Market Research

Although we have been discussing the importance of research all along, it will be prudent to further deep dive into the need to back up your product idea with extensive market research. After all, it is a crucial aspect of entrepreneurship since it helps validate the concept, understand the target audience, analyse competition and identify potential risks and opportunities, ultimately increasing the chances of success.

Market Size

In the 1989 American sports fantasy film, *Field of Dreams*, Ray Kinsella, a baseball fan and farmer (played by Kevin Costner) hears voices urging him to build a baseball field in his backyard. 'If you build it, he will come', said the voice. While businesses sometimes follow this adage, it is a risky proposition to say the least. You cannot build something in the hope that customers will follow. What you definitely need to ascertain is whether or not a market exists for your idea and what the potential market size is.

Odds are that you may have heard of three terms in this context, which can sound somewhat like an alphabet soup when you first hear them. Understood well, however, they can lend credence to your business plan. Here goes:

Total Addressable Market (TAM): This refers to the maximum size of the opportunity for a particular product or solution. In other words, it covers all possible users across the world who face problems that you are solving. In determining TAM, you are calculating that if every single person who could potentially find value in a product or solution purchased your product (that is, 100 per cent market share), how big would that market be? In calculating the TAM for bottled water, for instance, you would use the statistic of there being 7.5 billion people in the world with the recommended intake of 1.9 litres of water per day.

While TAM reflects the full market potential, realistically, no company can ever capture 100 per cent of the total available market. Why then is it important? Among other things, TAM offers you:

- Total market size and possible business growth
- A road map for product evaluation and competitiveness of the product
- The chance to put competitors in the line of sight early

Serviceable Addressable Market (SAM): This is the target addressable market that is served by a company's products or services. In other words, it is the part of TAM that you can serve at present.

So, for packaged drinking water, the SAM would be a subset of the world population, taking into account the regions where your product can be distributed and consumed. In calculating SAM, you might need to consider factors such as:

- **Geographical Limitations:** Only certain countries or regions where your product is available.
- **Market Demand:** Specific segments of the population that prefer packaged drinking water over other sources.
- **Competitive Landscape:** Areas where you can realistically compete with other packaged water brands.

Serviceable Obtainable Market (SOM): This is your go-to market focus group. This refers to the exact group of customers that form your target group in the short term.

For packaged drinking water, SOM would be a subset of SAM, considering the following factors:

- **Marketing and Sales Efforts:** How effective your marketing campaigns and sales teams are in reaching and converting potential customers.
- **Distribution Network:** The efficiency and reach of your distribution channels.
- **Brand Recognition and Loyalty:** The strength of your brand and customer loyalty in the target regions.
- **Competitive Position:** Your ability to compete with other brands in the market.

Let us take one more example to understand the concept of TAM, SAM & SOM further.

Imagine a company that is launching a new 'smart' pet collar that tracks a dog's activity and health data. Let us try to understand what the TAM, SAM and SOM in this example would comprise:

- **TAM (Total Addressable Market):**
  The entire global market for pet collars, including basic collars, which could be estimated as all dog owners worldwide, representing a very large market size.
- **SAM (Serviceable Available Market):**
  The portion of the pet collar market that this specific 'smart' collar could realistically target—dog owners in developed countries who are interested in advanced pet monitoring features and are willing to pay a premium price.
- **SOM (Serviceable Obtainable Market):**
  The smaller segment of the SAM that this company could realistically capture within a specific time

frame, considering factors including competition, marketing reach and brand recognition, which might be limited to dog owners in a particular region who are early adopters of tech-based pet products.

TAM, SAM and SOM are essential to business strategy as well as growth planning, since they reveal how big the opportunity is at every stage of business growth. Used well, they can help businesses arrive at viable niches. Needless to say, they are also important metrics that help present the value of your idea to potential investors. In fact, you will be able to win investor confidence if your business plan is in line with the SOM estimate.

User Validation

Having shortlisted a business idea and evaluated its market, the next logical step is to speak to potential users to actually check its veracity. While a start-up idea may have emerged from a problem a founder experiences himself, it is important to assess if others are equally troubled by it, a process that, in start-up parlance, is known as user validation.

To do that effectively, one has to begin with clearly defining who your target customer is. In fact, what you also need is a detailed representation of this consumer—what is known as building a consumer persona. It provides you with a clear picture of who you are building the product for, what problems they have, how they make decisions, what channels they use and more.

Building a consumer persona typically involves focusing on the following aspects:

- **Demographics**: Age, gender, income, education, occupation, geography, etc.
- **Psychographics**: Interests, values, lifestyle, attitudes, etc.
- **Behavioural patterns**: Purchasing habits, brand loyalty, online behaviour, etc.
- **Pain points**: Problems and challenges that the customer faces
- **Goals**: What the customer aims to achieve with your product or service

It is clear that in developing your customer personas, you need to focus on several aspects including the target segment's ability and willingness to pay for your product. If you are developing a discretionary product, for instance, odds are that Gen Z, the generation that is likely to splurge most on non-essential items, is among your key audience. Theirs represents an interesting psychology of living in the moment, which can be insightful for entrepreneurs.

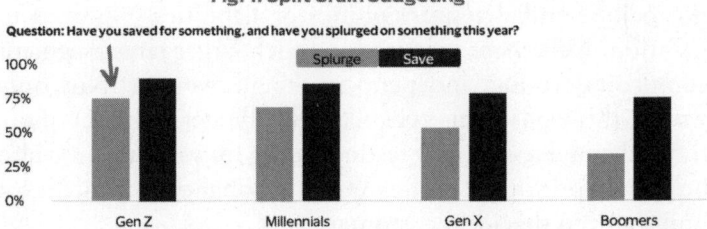

Fig. 1: Split-brain budgeting

Sources: Visa Business and Economic Insights analysis and CivicScience consumer survey, August 2023

While on the subject of Gen Z, another interesting aspect to note is that when it comes to their financing preferences, a major chunk of their expenses is financed by credit card usage on retail, travel and entertainment categories.

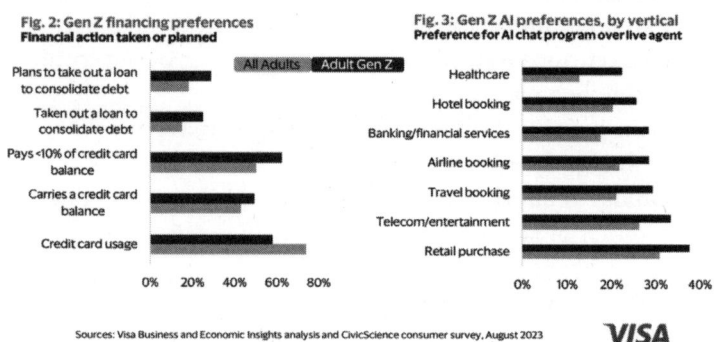

Sources: Visa Business and Economic Insights analysis and CivicScience consumer survey, August 2023

Getting back to the subject of building consumer personas, it will be worthwhile to look at some examples. When Tinder commenced operations in India, for instance, they may have defined the customer persona as a certain Neha Singh, a twenty-three-year-old female working in her first job, residing in Andheri East, Mumbai, single and independent and with no major familial responsibilities or liabilities. Needless to mention, Neha here represents a much larger target segment comprising young, independent, single women. Not only would this consumer persona help Tinder conduct more focused and relevant user testing, going forward it would also help them prioritize features and functionalities that are most important to this ideal customer.

Here is yet another detailed example of a consumer persona that you may find helpful.

DESCRIPTION	PSYCHOGRAPHICS	BEHAVIOUR PATTERNS
Kavya is a Marketing Professional who studied BA (Eco) at the University in Nagpur, and then did her MBA from Nirma Institute. She currently works in Mumbai at a D2C brand into feminine hygiene, draws a salary of Rs 1.7 Lakhs per month.	• **Values:** Career success, work-life balance, health & wellness • **Aspirations:** Professional advancement, finding a life partner, look youthful • **Personality:** Confident, independent, image-conscious, tech-savvy	• **Shopping:** Prefers premium brands, shops both online and in high-end stores • **Social Media:** Active on Instagram and LinkedIn • **Lifestyle:** Regular gym-goer, enjoys weekend brunches with friends
RECENT PURCHASES Spends over Rs 7k on beauty products monthly + Rs 3k at salon Bought a Dyson Hair Wrap Aqualogica Hydrating Face Cream Moxie Curly Hair Shampoo	**ASPIRATIONS** • Find a man who is fit + educated + lives by himself • Get married before 35 • Become CMO by 34	**CHALLENGES / INSECURITY** • Pigmentation / Wrinkles • Unable to find a match for over 4 years of search • Hair is wavy, but she likes straight – doesn't want rebonding
FAVORITE BRANDS Has iPhone, AirPods, MacBook Subko Coffee over Third Wave Uniqlo over Zara Has one fake LV bag + original Coach Wears a Tissot watch	**NEEDS** • Anti-frizz hair products • Under eye cream • Retinol and Niacinamide	**SOURCES OF INFO** • Beauty Influencers • Dermatologist Friend • Colleagues at the office

- 33 years old
- Mumbai
- Unmarried
- Marketing Director
- Family in Nagpur
- Rs 1.7 Lakh p.m.

The big advantage of developing a consumer persona is that, among other things, it keeps you away from the temptation of building a product for just about everyone. For when you build for all, remember you are really building for absolutely no one.

There is a very interesting story around this aspect that I absolutely love to tell. When TaxiForSure first launched, they were getting about eight rides per day. Until one day, data showed a happy anomaly—a huge peak of a single customer having taken as many as fifty-nine rides in a month. On digging deeper, it was found that the service was being availed by a pregnant lady who was using these rides to visit the doctor, attend yoga classes and more. The founders knew that they had hit on an important customer segment. In true start-up hustle fashion, the founders started visiting maternity hospitals at six every morning where they knew an important target group (TG) would be found. Speaking to this target group threw up some important insights. They found out that pregnant women were concerned about the driver not being rash while handling the car, not honking, keeping the AC on, not playing music, among other things. They then went on to build all those requirements as part of the standard operating procedure (SOP) to serve these customers better. That done, this target audience started using their service and the news spread across the entire community. Building for this TG saw their rides jump from eight to forty-five a day.

Theirs was a great example of the fact that when you enter a market, it will not be worth your while to care about getting a million customers who think you're decently okay. Instead it works far better if you can get 100 customers who love you, obsess about you and can't stop talking about you. This is not to say that you shouldn't gradually add more user personas; however, you need to be careful about building for everyone.

With the buyer personas in place, you now need to talk to your target segment first hand to validate the idea and unearth incisive insights. A few quick pointers worth remembering are:

- Use simple, conversational language to inquire; no jargon!
- Don't feed them the solution, build up towards it
- Gauge how big a problem they think it is
- Get a sense if they'd pay for your proposed solution
- Beware of your own biases, don't shrug away an opinion, because you personally don't agree with it
- Better still, have a conversation, not an interview

In particular, remember to steer clear of these three common pitfalls:

#1. Validating with the wrong users: Remember to validate the idea with users who are representative of your target segment. Not identifying your target audience correctly and trying to validate the idea with users who do not have the problem you are trying to solve can lead to false positives that could cost you dearly post launch.

#2. Asking leading questions: In the process of validating ideas with users, it is crucial not to ask leading questions that can influence the user's response. Open-ended questions that allow the user to give honest and useful feedback will work in your favour.

#3. Ignoring negative feedback: While it is extremely heartening to get positive feedback about your idea as it supports your start-up vision, it can prove to be fatal to ignore any negative feedback or push it under the carpet. Low ratings, high churn rates, low retention rates, negative comments—all are opportunities to improve your product or pivot your strategy. Failure to do it at this stage can prove to be extremely costly. On the other hand, a framework to prioritize the feedback can go a long way in developing a product that is in line with market requirements and expectations.

An important question to think about is also how many people is it prudent to survey? As a rule of thumb, the Margin of Error (MoE) in making any inferences from a survey, depending on the number of participants, is approximately 1/square root(N).

- At 10 respondents, your MoE therefore is at ~32 per cent
- At 100 respondents, the MoE drops to 10 per cent
- At 200, MoE is ~7 per cent
- At 500, MoE is ~4.5 per cent
- At 1000, MoE further drops to ~3 per cent

The above data shows that a sample size of less than 100 is likely to give you some incorrect inferences. On the other hand, the margin of error decreases only marginally with an increase in numbers beyond 200. It is best therefore to optimize for a respondent sample size to be between 100 and 200. While adding more respondents beyond this number will give you more accurate results (and possibly more credibility), the costs of conducting it may not justify the refinement in inference.

If you are undertaking large-scale research, I'd recommend taking professional help, especially if it's your first time. I am reminded of an anecdote that was narrated by Prof. Harish Bijoor in our Rural Marketing class at the Indian School of Business, Hyderabad, that I often quote.

How many pairs of underwear does an average Indian man own?

A consumer research company once went around asking Indian men this question. The answer they would invariably get is either three, four or five. However, when they entered the respondent's homes to identify those pairs, they found that an average Indian man had just 1.5 pairs of underwear. Companies that know their customers best are known to validate their insights through user observation, consumer behaviour understanding and history of ongoing consumer relationships to arrive at what would be a more refined consumer insight.

Minimum Viable Product (MVP)

It goes without saying that an even more dependable validation can be obtained only after consumers actually use or experience the solution you build. If people are willing to accept your solution and pay for it, you can be sure that you have identified a valid gap in the market.

This brings us to yet another important concept that can help us gain user validation: the concept of a Minimum Viable Product or an MVP. To put it simply, an MVP is a basic version of your product. If one had to define two characteristics of an MVP, they would have to be speed and frugality. What this means is that you need to be able to develop an MVP quickly and without spending too much money on it. Take, for instance, the example of Goodreads, the world's largest site and app for readers and book recommendations. What in your opinion would be the MVP for Goodreads? A WhatsApp group of book lovers where every member reviews their choice of book, did I hear you say? This is the way most start-ups begin, catering to a small set of the target audience. What is important to note here is also the fact that the MVP of a product isn't something that can scale; it is not meant to. Its objective is simply to validate whether or not the simplified version of the product has takers at a small scale.

A word of caution here. It may so happen that the problem is validated by users, yet the product fails to gain traction. If you happen to encounter such a situation, you need to work at understanding the exact pain points of the consumer—whether it is cost, quality, convenience or any other—and make changes to the offered product. In the absence of this exercise, you may need to make painful, large-scale changes at an advanced stage.

I would recommend that you read *The Lean Startup* by Eric Ries, which acts as a comprehensive guide to building and using MVPs.

Product-Market Fit (PMF)

'When a great team meets a lousy market, the market wins. When a lousy team meets a great market, the market wins. When a great team meets a great market, something special happens.'

The above quote, attributed to Andy Rachleff, a venture capitalist, was later popularized by Marc Andreessen, co-founder of Netscape, in his discussions about the importance of what is known as a product-market fit, an oft-used jargon in the start-up space.

Marc Andreessen, in fact, is considered to be one of the pioneers of PMF. He described PMF as being in a good market with a product that can satisfy the market. Essentially then, you can say that you have achieved a product market fit when a lot of people are willing to pay for the product and you aren't struggling to acquire users. In an ideal scenario, this means that your customers are spreading the word about your product and that your marketing spends are nominal.

Typically, finding PMF involves going through the following stages:

1. Determine your target customer
2. Identify underserved customer needs
3. Define your value proposition
4. Specify your MVP feature set
5. Create your MVP prototype
6. Test your MVP with customers

These stages crossed, when can you say with certainty that you have, in fact, achieved PMF? Sean Ellis, a well-known growth hacking expert, came up with an interesting '40 per cent test' that can be useful in ascertaining PMF. Simply put, the rule states that if more than 40 per cent of your users were to feel 'Very Disappointed' if your product was to vanish tomorrow, it is a strong indicator that you are close to PMF. Of course, implied in this metric is the fact that you should have at least a few hundred users if not a few thousand, for the 40 per cent rule to be a robust indicator.

Yet another metric that can be indicative of PMF is something known as the Net Promoter Score (NPS). The score indicates customer satisfaction and measures how many users are also your promoters. To calculate it, a customer survey asks customers to score on a scale of 0–10 (where 0 means not at all and 10 means most definitely) how likely they are to recommend the product or service to someone they know.

Customers are then classified as below basis their scores:

0 to 6: Detractors
7 to 8: Neutrals
9 to 10: Promoters
NPS = % of Promoters - % of Detractors
A score of 30 and above is considered great and is an indicator of PMF.

Product-Market-Founder-Fit

While PMF is a key determinant of the success of a product, there is yet another metric that ensures the product will sustain beyond the PMF. This aspect, known as the Product–Market–Founder Fit (PMFF), refers to the alignment between a company's product offering, the market it serves and the skills, experience and passion of the founder. It determines whether or not the founder(s) is suitable to lead the growth and evaluation of the product. To a large extent, it boils down to the motivation of the founder to build right. Some of the aspects that can be indicative of PMFF often are whether or not the founder has a personal experience with the problem, whether the founder has extensive experience and insight of the industry and, most importantly, whether he has the intrinsic motivation to build a start-up. We spoke about the entrepreneurial mindset in detail earlier in the book. That, of course, has a huge role to play in the founder being able to solve many problems that are likely to present themselves along the way.

While PMFF isn't spoken about as much as PMF, it is what spurs the founder to drive the product to PMF and beyond it.

Section Three

Business Planning and Set-Up

- Go-to-Market Strategy; Distribution—B2B, B2C, B2B2C, B2G
- Branding and Marketing
- Team: Co-founders, Early Skills, ESOPs
- Finance: P&L, Balance Sheet, Cash Flow Statement

Having zeroed in on a business idea, you need to go the whole way; whether it is figuring out your go-to-market strategy or creating an organizational structure. These are among the many areas that we will explore in this section as we focus on the nuances of actually launching a business.

Go-to-Market Strategy

The idea and product validation done, you already have a hypothesis in place about which customers you'd look to acquire first. It is now time to plan your Go-to-Market Strategy—the 'how' of acquiring these customers. This, of course, involves identifying avenues to reach them in the most cost-effective manner possible.

For one, you need to work at your distribution strategy. There are various modes of distribution that a founder can approach in making his products reach his end customers.

B2C and B2B channels of distribution

If your product needs to be sold to individual consumers, you will take to the Business-to-Consumer (B2C) model. It is, in fact, the most common form of transaction that we encounter in our daily lives. Think about when you buy clothes online from a company's website, order food via delivery apps or subscribe to a streaming service. All these interactions are examples of B2C transactions.

From the business standpoint, however, customer acquisition in a B2C business is typically an expensive affair. A chunk of a company's budget is spent in customer acquisition, as well as in long-term brand building. Popular brands, in fact, are known to have burnt a lot of cash to acquire customers.

On the other hand, if, as a business, you are selling your products directly to other businesses, typically involving channels like wholesalers, distributors, online marketplaces and more without selling directly to consumers, you would be making use of a B2B distribution model.

Depending upon the product category, of course, I recommend that founders first sell to businesses directly (B2B) and in time, with enough capital and experience, cater to the B2C segment. By the time the company has matured in the B2B segment, there will be easier entry into the B2C network as the company would have an established brand name and better access to distribution and raw material.

That said, there are enough and more examples of successful companies that started out in the B2C space and now are making significant forays into the B2B market.

Forest Essentials, for instance, is a well-known luxury beauty brand. Though one can purchase their range of skin and hair care products from their on-site stores or from other sites like Nykaa, they have also developed partnerships with some of India's leading five-star hotel chains. This is an example of a B2C company now focusing on B2B growth.

B2B2B and B2B2C Distribution

B2B2B (Business-to-Business-to-Business)

Tally is a well-known accounting software product. The company realized that chartered accountants (CAs) held tremendous influence over their sales. If the CA recommends Tally, the client usually buys it. With this insight, the company began to share referral codes with CAs and kept track of how many new customers they brought in. By doing so, they created a B2B2B distribution network and their presence today is unmatched in the Indian market.

By definition then, a B2B2B company sells its products/services to another business, which then uses them to serve other businesses.

Key features of such a model include:

- Multiple layers of business relationships
- Typically longer sales cycles
- Complex value chains
- Specialized or technical products often
- Higher transaction values

Some more examples of B2B2B sales include:

1. Chip manufacturers (like TSMC) → Device manufacturers (like Intel) → Computer companies (like Dell)

2. Raw material suppliers → Manufacturing equipment makers → Factory operators
3. Cloud infrastructure providers (like Amazon Web Services) → Software companies → Business clients

B2B2C (Business-to-Business-to-Consumer)

A financing business partners with a home appliance manufacturer to offer loans to customers when they purchase a home appliance. The financing firm benefits from the partnership by acquiring end consumers for its loan services. What you are seeing in action is a B2B2C model.

By definition then, a B2B2C model is a combination of B2B and B2C models. The parent B2B company onboards multiple sellers/vendors as its partners and leverages its partners' strength, market presence and customer base.

Key features of a B2B2C model include:

- Direct connection to end consumers through intermediary businesses
- Usually faster sales cycles than B2B2B
- Focus on consumer experience
- Often involves white-labelling or co-branding
- Emphasis on marketing and user interface

Examples of B2B2C models include:

1. Payment processors (like Stripe) → Online retailers → Shoppers
2. Food suppliers → Restaurants → Diners
3. Insurance underwriters → Insurance agents → Policyholders

It will also be worthwhile to look at some of the key differences between B2B and B2C models. These relate to:

1. **End Customer**
   As seen above, in the case of a B2B2B business, the final consumer is a business. This is as opposed to a B2B2C model where the final customer is the end consumer.
2. **Value Chain Complexity**
   A B2B2B generally follows a more complex value chain as opposed to a B2B2C business that is more streamlined and focuses on the user experience.
3. **Sales Process**
   Typically, a B2B2B business is likely to witness longer sales cycles with multiple decision-makers. B2B2C businesses, on the other hand, have a quicker sales cycle with more emphasis on scalability.
4. **Marketing Approach**
   As far as the marketing approach goes, a B2B2B model is driven by a lot of technical specifications and a strong Return on Investment (ROI) focus. The marketing approach of a B2B2C business, on the other hand, is driven by consumer benefits and brand awareness.
5. **Price Points**
   Typically a B2B2B model follows a usually higher, more complex pricing while for a B2B2C business, the pricing is more standardized and consumer-friendly.

What about B2G?

Besides the B2B and B2C models and their extensions, there is yet another specialized model applicable to businesses selling products, services or solutions directly to government agencies and public sector organizations. The model deserves a special mention especially since procuring business from government agencies comes with its own unique aspects. For one, it often requires businesses to participate in a bidding process or submit proposals to win contracts. Businesses are also required to comply with strict regulations, standards and requirements set by government agencies. On the positive side, B2G transactions often involve long-term contracts and stable, recurring revenue streams for businesses. Examples of B2G sales include companies that produce electronics/equipment/arms/anti-drone software and more that cater to the defence sector.

Go ahead and evaluate the distribution channels that will work for your business taking into account your target audience, nature of product, channel performance, among other aspects.

Branding and Marketing

While an effective MVP can get you to your first few users, scaling beyond that will require you to crack not only the distribution game but also invest in marketing. Far from a spray-and-pray approach, effective marketing involves tracking relevant metrics as you try to gain a foothold in the market.

While we tend to think of marketing spend as one homogenous whole, it can be potentially divided into three heads:

a) **Ad Spend on Customer Acquisition**: As its name suggests, this is the marketing spend that you incur with the goal of acquiring new customers. We are going to look at the important metric of Customer Acquisition Costs (CAC) that helps track this spend, in some detail shortly.

b) **Ad Spend on Performance Marketing**: This is the money you spend on ads with the goal of getting more sale orders or paid subscriptions. The metric to be tracked here is known as Return on Ad Spend (ROAS).
c) **Ad Spend on Branding**: These are ads that you run for visibility, awareness and positioning. Typically, such ads may not have a clear call to action. Ads such as those on billboards, magazines, television or different mobile apps are often run with the purpose of brand enhancement.

Let us look at the metrics associated with each of these spends in some detail.

Customer Acquisition Costs (CAC)

As discussed, this is the money spent in order to get a consumer to download your app, for instance. A very basic way of calculating CAC is dividing your marketing spend by the number of new users onboarded. If you spend Rs 1 lakh on marketing in a certain period and get 1000 users to register on your app, your CAC is Rs 100000/1000 users—or a CAC of Rs 100.

It is important to mention here that in the above example, what we are looking at is the Blended CAC, since we have considered the overall marketing spend on different channels. It will help to further break down the marketing spend and calculate the CAC for each of the different marketing channels, namely, Facebook, Instagram, Google Ads, Influencer Marketing and more. While the blended CAC tells you the overall efficacy of your consumer acquisition efforts, the individual CAC tells you of the efficacy of each channel.

While talking about CAC, it is also important to remember that there are some users who would onboard organically, without any marketing spend. The better the paid-to-organic user ratio, the lower the CAC.

Several start-ups incur high CAC in the hope that customers thus acquired will become active users and over the lifetime of their association with the product, generate profits that will far outweigh the CAC. This brings us to yet another metric, that of Lifetime Value of a customer or LTV.

LTV refers to the total profits that a customer generates for a start-up over a lifetime.

LTV = Average CM* per order x total number of orders over the lifetime

As an example, if you order on the food delivery app Swiggy eighteen times in a year and if the average contribution margin across your orders is Rs 20, your LTV, assuming that you will remain their customer for ten years, is 20 x 18 x 10 = Rs 3600.

As a thumb rule, an LTV to CAC ratio of 3 or above is usually considered acceptable.

Return on Ad Spend (ROAS)

While the amount that you spend on customer acquisition enables you to acquire a user, this user may or may not be a spending customer. It is the money spent on performance marketing that is aimed at selling your product or, in other words, acquiring paid users. The metric that measures it is known as Return on Ad Spend (ROAS). It is simply

---

* Contribution Margin (means profit after removing known variable costs and before deducting any overheads or fixed costs). Variable costs include raw materials, packaging, labour, etc., that are directly correlated to the number of units produced.

calculated by dividing the revenue generated by the total ad spend. Let's say you spend Rs 100 on advertising and your campaign results in Rs 150 of sales—your ROAS will be 1.5. In other words, you earn Rs 1.5 for every Re 1 that you spend on advertising. Many marketers consider 4:1 a threshold for a good ROAS.

A more effective way of calculating ROAS, however, is dividing the total contribution margin (or the profit component) by the Total Ad Spend.

Broadly, it is noted that ROAS is high initially as early adopters buy even without much ad spend. With time, however, ROAS can start to plateau.

Measuring Brand Marketing

Before we get to the metrics of brand marketing, let us spend a little time understanding some aspects of it.

Branding essentially is the process of creating a unique identity for a product, service or company in the mind of consumers. It's how you convey your brand values, personality and what makes you different from your competitors. Effective branding helps to build recognition, trust and loyalty among customers. For example, luxury brands like BMW and Dior can command a higher price due to the perception the brand carries.

An important strategy of branding is what is known as brand laddering. In this approach, the key functional attributes of a product are highlighted first and higher-order benefits are subsequently introduced to win over target consumers so they are willing to pay for the product. As per Prof. Kevin Keller, 'Brand laddering involves progression from attributes to benefits to more abstract values or motivations.' While product utility is a must, founders must also focus on design, experience, storytelling, community building, cultural relevance, etc., to make the product succeed in the long run and establish a loyal customer base. An example of brand laddering for Coca-Cola is shared below:

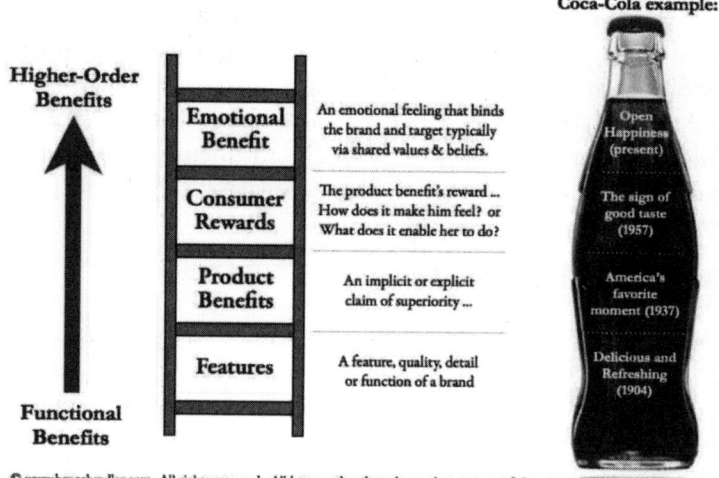

Besides building a strong brand, the business also benefits from the founder having a personal brand that helps in humanizing the business as also building relatability with the target audience.

While it may be grossly unfair to suggest that the rise in the value of brands such as boAt, Mamaearth or Sugar Cosmetics is on account of the founders' appearance on *Shark Tank* (because it would undermine the years of hard work and grit that they've put in), it's a fact that building a personal brand helps a great deal.

All of this brings us to the question: How does one measure the efficacy of branding? While there may not be a way to directly ascertain how that hoarding of your brand or its corporate campaign has impacted sales, branding goes a long way in increasing the recall value. Impacted by your brand campaign, when the customer goes to buy a product the next time around, chances are that your brand will have top-of-mind recall. Additionally, brand marketing is seen to improve the conversion rate of performance marketing.

Viral Coefficient

As a founder, what you want to do at the fundamental level, is to ensure that your product is used by the maximum number of people while you make minimal spends on marketing. This can be done by ensuring what is known as a high viral coefficient.

In order to drive this coefficient, businesses often run referral campaigns. Think of brands like Cult.fit, which offer you a fifteen-day service free of cost, should a friend sign up on its app using your referral code. A company like Tally similarly shares referral codes with chartered accountants and tracks how many new customers they bring.

Viral coefficient can be calculated as under:

Viral coefficient = Number of users * % of users who have referred * % conversion

Team: Co-Founders, Early Skills, ESOPs

Much as you need to focus on product availability, marketing and more, a start-up requires equal focus on its internal composition. In fact, a great founding team is perhaps the single-most important marker of a business's success. Conversely, among all things involved in setting up a business, co-founder conflict is believed to be the number one reason for a start-up's failure. Intelligence and ability aside, it stands to reason that if you can't work well with your co-founders, your start-up will not see much success.

Even before we get to understand the co-founder dynamics crucial to a start-up's health, a good place to begin will be to determine whether or not you even need a co-founder. Ali Tamaseb's research (Tamaseb is a venture capitalist and the author of the book, *Super Founders*) on the number of co-founders in billion-dollar start-ups found that there wasn't a direct correlation between the number of co-founders and the start-up's success. His research of 195 start-ups that became unicorns between 2005 and 2018 in the US, found that about 20 per cent of them had just one founder, 35 per cent had two and 30 per cent had three, while the rest had four or more founders.[*]

In a 2016 article on TechCrunch by Haje Jan Kamps, however, data of 7348 companies that had raised at least $10 million in funding showed that almost 46 per cent of those start-ups had a single founder, almost 32 per cent had two and 15 per cent had three.

If we consider both these data sets to be true, it appears as if a higher number of solo-founded companies are able to raise at least $10 million in funding, but from among them, chances of further becoming a unicorn are highest for start-ups with two co-founders followed by three.

Perks of Having a Co-founder

The above data apart, let us look at some of the reasons why having a co-founder or two may be beneficial.

First things first, building a start-up isn't an easy process by any stretch of the imagination. Not only is the success rate low, you are dealing with a whole lot of known and

---

[*] Haje Jan Kamps, 'Breaking a myth: Data shows you don't actually need a co-founder', TechCrunch, 26 August 2016, https://techcrunch.com/2016/08/26/co-founders-optional/.

'unknown unknowns' that tend to take a toll on you mentally and emotionally. Having a partner on this ride makes the process that much easier, which can otherwise feel extremely isolating.

With co-founder(s) in place who have different competencies, the burden of handling myriad things also reduces substantially. When a builder and a seller get together for instance, with product development and sales as their core competencies, the ride becomes that much easier.

With start-ups beginning their journey largely in the bootstrapped mode, one or more co-founders also means that the load of investments is distributed. It is not uncommon to see that one of the co-founders even continues working in a regular job while the other works at the start-up full time, until it scales.

The above said, there are, of course, scenarios when going solo can make sense. For instance, if a product has been built by a founder and it has found paying customers with its MVP, the solo founder may not feel the pressing need of having a co-founder. Similarly, if the solo founder has enough funds to set the ball rolling, he may not want to have a co-founder early on. In such cases, the founder may find it more prudent to appoint a founding team to be able to delegate jobs. In some cases, founders confess that despite their best efforts, they are not able to find the right co-founder, who could complement their skills and whom they find a fitment with. In such cases, it wouldn't be wise to rush into a co-founder relationship. Much like a marriage, the wrong co-founder relationship can lead to several conflicts that can even end up with the business shutting down. So, it may be best to run the business yourself along with an able team, till the right co-founder comes along.

Should you decide to go with a co-founder, it will be worthwhile to look for complementary skills. A tech start-up, for instance, will benefit from a builder and a seller, just as an AI-based SaaS product will probably require both an AI expert and a software developer to build it right. Similarly, manufacturing-based start-ups may require one person to supervise the operational aspects of manufacturing while another manages the R&D for the product.

Before considering a third co-founder for your start-up, it will always be worthwhile to check whether that person is coming in with a complementary skill set that is indeed adding value and will increase the speed and efficiency.

A word of caution here. While it is easier to find a co-founder whose competencies fit the bill on paper, it is equally important that there is a meeting of minds in terms of their ambition, goals and aspirations, ethics and overall rapport. After all, you cannot spend day after gruelling day with someone at work whom you don't identify with and worse still, don't like. It will help you, among other things, to determine what your motivation for starting up is. Big chasms of difference in motivation sometimes can signal the end of a start-up. For instance, if one co-founder's motivation to start up is for social purposes while for the other it is money alone, you could well be staring at a rocky road. However, even with differing motivations, it can work well if the co-founders are able to openly discuss them, play out different scenarios well in advance and look for common ground.

Investors too are known to pay a fair amount of attention to co-founder fitment when assessing a start-up for investment. Other than complementary skills, if, for instance, they see a past working relationship, it often becomes a good indicator of the fact that chances of interpersonal and professional conflict are lower. This is not to say that long-term relationships cannot break down, especially in the face of overwhelming pressure. However, the odds are that much better.

Equity Split

That brings us to an important question of what an optimum equity split between founders should be. While it is common to witness an equal equity split between co-founders, there are several scenarios that demand an unequal split. These include:

- Joining the start-up at different times
- Difference in investments in the company
- Difference in experience or expertise
- Difference in salaries drawn
- If the product under development is based on a patented intellectual property (IP) owned by one of the co-founders

The underlying principle to follow, of course, is that the equity split should be fair enough to keep the founders engaged and motivated.

Finding and Compensating Advisers

Ever so often, you may also need to look for advisers in your business. This may happen particularly if you are unable to find a suitable co-founder or even otherwise, when the business is in need of strategic advice. For instance, you may feel the need for an industry expert at the ideation stage of the start-up. Similarly, you may need to reach out to an adviser at the MVP stage to help you build the product. Entrepreneurs often feel the need to look for advisers to guide them through the fundraising process, as also in periods of brand building and growth.

While advisers are often paid a fee, at times, you may also allot them advisory equity in the start-up. Needless to say, the allocation of advisory equity should be preceded by a well-thought-out plan of the kind of value they are likely to add. In fact, I advise founders to be highly protective of their equity and to use cash wherever possible and feasible.

As a thumb rule, the adviser pool in total should ideally not exceed 2 per cent of the total shareholding of the company. While allocating equity, it is also best to link it to achievement of certain milestones.

The Founder Adviser Standard Template (FAST) prescribed by the Founder Institute (fi.co), a founder education and networking platform, can offer a useful template with regard to the points to negotiate and terms to agree on, before onboarding advisers.

Employee Stock Option Plans (ESOPs)

Often, especially in the early stages of the start-up, founders are constrained in offering market salaries to their key hires. In such a situation, ESOPs come in handy to attract talent. As the start-up grows, of course, employees who have stayed and contributed to its growth also need to be compensated fairly through the ESOP option. Essentially, ESOPs ensure a sufficient partaking of employees in the start-up's profits. Overall, ESOPs are crucial for aligning employee and company interests, boosting retention and incentivizing long-term performance, offering both financial benefits and a sense of ownership to employees.

Start-ups, therefore, need to set up an ESOP pool to be distributed among their key hires. Remember, however, that issuing ESOPs does not immediately offer equity to the employee. It only means that they have the right to claim a stake in the future, subject to certain criteria. Let us look at some important aspects of ESOPs:

The first thing to figure out is, of course, who are the employees eligible for ESOPs. Eligibility of ESOPs can be linked to factors such as their time of joining, performance, criticality of role, seniority and more. Having identified the eligible employees, you would issue them a grant letter, which is a legal document that lists the terms and conditions of the ESOP policy.

Vesting Period

A very important term linked to granting of ESOPs to employees is the vesting period. This refers to the length of time the employee must spend with the company to earn the right to exercise the ESOPs in full. Essentially, it acts as a tool to incentivize employees to stay with the company longer. For example, if an employee is eligible for 100 ESOPs, the vesting period may be four years where the employee earns 25 per cent of the ESOPs at the end of year one to four, respectively. Vesting, however, may also take place in a staggered manner, where the vesting schedule may follow a 10-20-30-40 vesting schedule, for instance.

In the context of ESOPs, you may have also heard of the term 'cliff'. It refers to the minimum period an employer needs to be employed with the company to earn any ESOPs at all. One year is a standard most companies tend to follow.

As an example, let us assume that an employee possesses 100 stock options with a vesting period of four years and a cliff of one year. After the first year is complete, twenty-five of these stock options get vested. Now, the employee has an option to convert these options to shares or, in other words, to exercise their options. Vested ESOPs, if not exercised, may be extinguished if the ESOP policy defines a timeline for mandatory exercising of ESOPs. However, if there is no such timeline, then such vested ESOPs may remain vested, to be exercised immediately before a liquidation event, such as an IPO or an acquisition of the company, when all shareholders get money in return for their shares.

Exercise Price

The exercise price is the price an employee needs to pay to buy their vested shares.

This is the discounted share price, usually a nominal value, decided by the company at the time of issuance of the ESOPs and mentioned in the ESOP grant letter. This price depends on the fair market value of the shares at the time they are being granted.

What should be the size of the ESOP pool?

This is a basic question that entrepreneurs often contend with. In calculating the ESOP pool, some entrepreneurs tend to go by 'industry norms'. It may, however, work better to calculate the ESOP pool by dividing your manpower cost by the post-money value of your start-up.

We are going to keep coming back to many of these issues once we get to the funding journey of the start-up.

Finance: P&L, Balance Sheet, Cash Flow Statement

As you begin to transact business, you need to learn to keep a keen eye on the company's financial health. While founders sometimes shy away from finances and accounting, the fact is that you need to be well versed in understanding and reading your company's accounting statements. In the initial days, in any case, complexities are minimal and a basic knowledge of finance can help you keep track.

Let us begin with a broad understanding of three basic accounting statements:

- Profit & Loss Statement
- Balance Sheet
- Cash Flow Statement

P&L Statement

Simply put, this statement tells you how profitable (or not) your business is. Let us look at the line items that make up the P&L statement.

The first line item and the most precious one for an entrepreneur, of course, is the revenue. Referred to as the top line, it is the total money that comes into the business through its sales. A business could have multiple revenue streams, in which case the break-up of this revenue is also captured.

A word of caution here. While it is common to use the terms total sales and revenue interchangeably, total sales generated isn't always equivalent to the revenue. In the case of marketplaces, for instance, the sales that they undertake on behalf of multiple brands is what is known as Gross Merchandise Value (GMV), which isn't equal to the revenue generated by the marketplace for itself. Revenues for them comprise the commissions they make out of sales. For D2C brands, on the other hand, the sales and GMV can be used interchangeably. As a thumb rule, revenue is the final amount that the company receives in its bank account after incurring any commissions, transaction costs, etc., on sales.

The next line item is the variable costs. This is also often listed as cost of goods sold (COGS). Usually, entrepreneurs tend to include only the direct material costs under this head, but ideally, it should also include all the other variable costs associated with the product. Let us take an example. Say, you are in the business of selling cricket bats. To get 1000 bats made, you pay Rs 10 lakh to a manufacturer. You incur another Rs 2 lakh on the packaging of these bats. The COGS in this case is Rs 12 lakh and the COGS per unit is Rs 1200.

While we are on the subject, it will also be worthwhile to understand two other oft-used metrics: Gross Margin and Contribution Margin.

Simply put, gross margin is calculated by deducting the COGS from the revenue. In the above example, if you decide to sell each bat at Rs 5000, your gross margin is 5000-1200 = 3800.

As for the contribution margin, it is the actual profit that you make on each sale. It is calculated by subtracting the direct variable costs from revenue.

The contribution margin can be calculated at different levels. For instance:

- Contribution Margin 1 (CM1): Net Sales - COGS. This is what is also commonly referred to as Gross Margin
- Contribution Margin 2 (CM2): CM1 - Fulfilment Costs (for example, shipping, transaction fees)
- Contribution Margin 3 (CM3): CM2 - Marketing Spend

As you can see, the contribution margin must be positive for the business to make real economic sense.

In the above example, if your contribution margin is 5 per cent, you would be making Rs 190 as profit on each bat sold. Go back and also link this to the concept of CAC we spoke about earlier. If your CAC is Rs 100, for instance, you would have more than recovered the CAC in this single sale.

Next on the P&L statement, you need to account for the fixed costs. These are costs that a business incurs irrespective of the volumes produced and sold. This includes salaries, rent, utilities, among others.

After you deduct the fixed costs from CM2, you will arrive at the operating profits of EBITDA.

It is important to note that operating profits do not take into account interest, taxes, depreciation and amortization since they do not have much to do with business operations. Interest, for instance, is dependent on how the capital of the business is structured and not on business performance. Similarly, taxation varies on factors that have little to do with operations. Depreciation and amortization are also dependent on a number of non-quantifiable factors. They do not have any direct significance on day-to-day operations and are rightfully kept aside from the calculation of operating profits or EBITDA.

Balance Sheet

The next and very important accounting statement to look at is the Balance Sheet. In basic terms, the balance sheet shows what a company owns on the one hand and what it owes on the other.

The two main components of the balance sheet are its assets and liabilities. Let us look at each of them in some detail.

Liabilities

It includes what a business owes to others. Liabilities have two segments: capital or shareholder's funds and borrowed funds.

Shareholder's funds is the money that shareholders have invested in the company. Shareholder's funds, in turn, can be of three types:

- **Equity Shareholder's Fund**: What the founders invest as equity. In bootstrapped businesses, these funds are often put in by founders from their personal savings
- **Preferred Stock**: Refers to investments of angels or VC investors
- **Reserves and Surplus**: Refers to accumulated profits of a business on the given date

Borrowed funds, as the name suggests, is what you have borrowed from other people. This is further classified as long-term borrowing, such as loans taken from a bank for a period of at least twelve months, and short-term borrowing, which are loans taken for short-term needs.

Assets

Assets are simply what the company owns. Assets may be long term or short term. Long-term assets are those that are expected to benefit the company for a number of years. Short-term assets, on the other hand, are held for a year or less and are expected to be converted to cash within this period. Cash in the bank is also an example of a short-term asset. Short-term assets also include account receivables or the money that is yet to be received after the sale of a product or service.

Cash Flow Statement

Last but not least, let us look at the Cash Flow Statement that helps you understand how much cash your company received and spent in a given period. Do keep in mind that a cash flow statement is distinct from the company's profits. While profit is the notional money left with the business after taking into account all the expenses, cash flow indicates the net flow of cash into and out of the business.

A cash flow statement, in turn, has three components:

Operating Cash Flow: It measures the cash generated from regular business operations

Cash Flow from Financing Activities: It tracks the net change in cash flow used for funding activities, namely, equity or debt

Cash Flow from Investing Activities: Tracks the cash spent or generated on investing activities.

While the above concepts are a drop in the ocean in the financial metrics to be tracked by entrepreneurs, it is imperative that you know these basics to have a fair understanding of the company's financial health.

Section Four

Funding Fundamentals

- When and How Much to Raise
- Sources of Finance: Debt vs Equity
- Stages of Equity Funding
- How to Value Your Business

Mention the term 'funding' and odds are that the images that it conjures are of newspaper headlines that scream large funding rounds and the making of a 'unicorn'. With a show like *Shark Tank* having brought entrepreneurship to the mainstream in India and legitimizing this career path, you could also be manifesting the high of an 'All Shark Deal'.

Much as the start-up ecosystem is replete with positive stories of raising funds and creating disproportionate value, there are cautionary tales as well. In fact, just as I sit to write this segment on funding, the shocking and disheartening news of the Blusmart-Gensol financial mismanagement has rocked the start-up world. This isn't really the story of one celebrated company's fall from grace, it's a mirror held up to the entire ecosystem—one where we need to be careful not to trade integrity for image.

It is important, therefore, to begin by thinking what your fundraising goals really are. As long as your fundraising goal isn't vanity, the following section will help you with actionable insights on things to do across your fundraising journey.

That said, let us begin at the very beginning. While securing start-up capital is a founder's dream moment, the funding avenues can differ significantly for micro, small, and medium enterprises (MSMEs) vs start-ups. The journey is best begun by understanding the difference between the two.

MSMEs vs Start-ups

While both start-ups and MSMEs can be entrepreneurial ventures, the key difference lies in their growth orientation and purpose. While start-ups are known to focus on rapid, disruptive growth and innovation, MSMEs aim for steady, sustainable growth within established industries. If we were to get a little more into the specifics, the key differences lie in terms of the following aspects:

	MSME	**Start-up**
Enabler	Arbitrage	Tech and Data
Market	Perfect Competition	Duopoly and Winner Take All
Profitability	Immediate	Deferred
Differentiator	Cost/Quality	Tech Innovation
Financing	Typically Bootstrapped	External Equity
Risk	Low	High

	MSME	**Start-up**
Reward	Low	High
Growth	Predictable	Hockey Stick

Having run through the above table, you surely would be thinking of several start-ups and mentally recognizing how their USP rests on a tech innovation and that their business model fits the high risk-high reward framework. Think of an MSME, on the other hand, and you will notice that they thrive on more traditional business enablers and work on a low risk-low reward model. If we were to plot a start-up and an MSME on the business model and scalability quadrants, you will notice that they lie on the opposite ends of the spectrum.

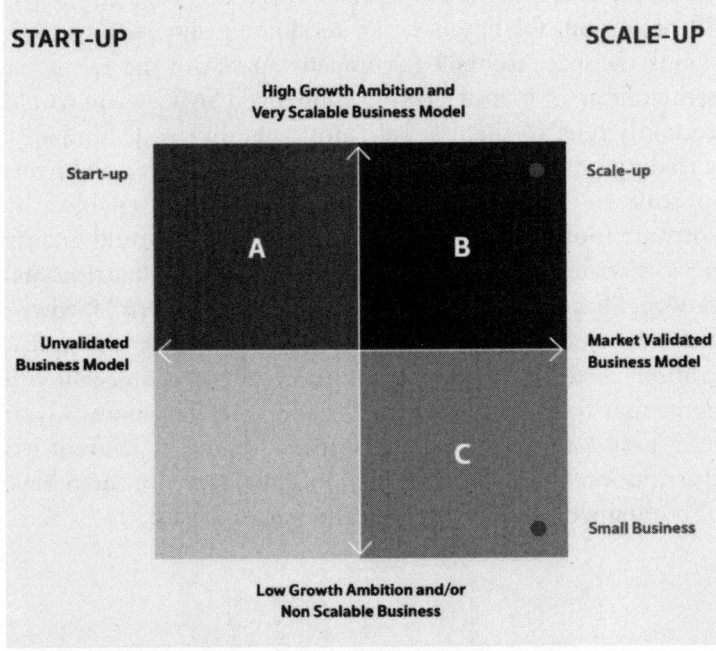

On the basis of the differences highlighted above, it will also be interesting to see if certain businesses/industries naturally align themselves towards being referred to as start-ups, while some others as MSMEs. Sectors such as software and SaaS, e-commerce marketplaces, for instance, are home to a number of start-ups. On the other hand, manufacturing businesses with their high capex and low margins would definitely classify as MSME, as would trading businesses that play on arbitrage. Service businesses that are known for their high margins yet low scalability, similarly, would be regarded as MSME.

Does this mean that a manufacturing, trading or service business cannot qualify as a start-up at all? Well, life is seldom so watertight. The answer to that question, therefore, is a resounding no. A manufacturing business that can innovate on its product and process, enabled by cutting-edge R&D and IP protection, for instance, can certainly qualify as a start-up. Think the space technology company SpaceX or the Taiwanese semiconductor manufacturing company TSMC—you would certainly refer to them as start-ups, wouldn't you? Similarly, a trading or services business that connects sellers and buyers at scale or solves for information asymmetry enabled by software tools and/or real time data processing would qualify as a start-up. Think of the popular online matrimonial service, Shaadi.com; the online investment platform, Groww; the home services platform, Urban Company; the quick commerce service company, Blinkit and more, and you will agree that they make the cut. What about D2C brands, you ask? Enabled by unique distribution channels, content-led distribution and data trends and insights, many of them have also obtained a firm footing in the start-up space.

You surely would recognize many powerful D2C start-ups in the rather thickly populated graphic below:

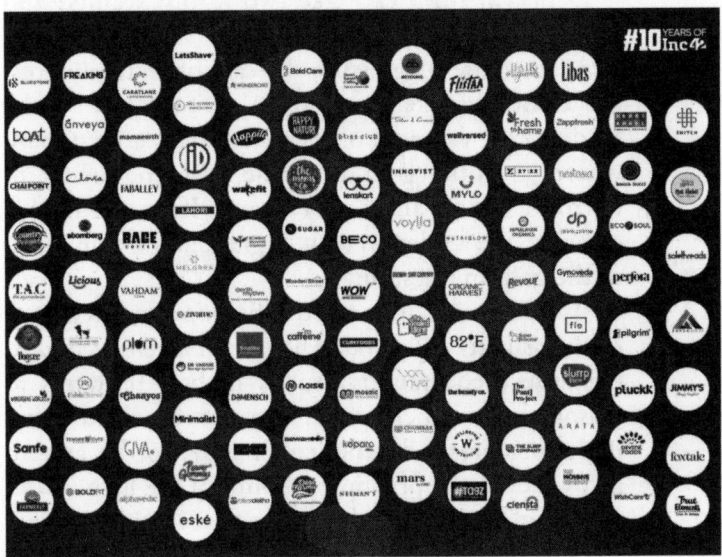

Sources of Finance

That differentiation made, let us continue on our funding journey and discuss the various sources of funding available to a start-up.

Start-up funding can take two primary forms: Debt and Equity. Let's quickly understand how each of them works.

a. **Debt Financing**
   Debt financing simply means that one borrows funds from another entity—an individual, a bank or any other institution—with a promise to return that money over a specified period with a certain interest. As is typical of any debt, regardless of the business' performance, the borrower is obligated to repay the

money due within a given timeframe. All types of loans fall under debt financing.

Debts, in turn, can take two forms: secured and unsecured.

As its name suggests, in the case of secured debts, the borrower offers a security or collateral to the lender. One example of secured debt is a gold loan, where you offer gold as collateral to the lender to borrow a certain amount of money. If you are unable to repay, the lender, in turn, is granted the ownership of the gold in question.

With regard to unsecured debt, you aren't required to furnish any collateral. The rate of interest charged for unsecured loans is usually higher. It stands to reason—since there are no assets involved—that if the business fails, the lender may not be able to recover even the principal amount of the loan.

When one needs a loan, the first institution that comes to mind is a bank. However, banks are often unwilling to fund start-ups due to the high risk of failure. Also, banks usually offer secured debts. Since start-ups do not always have tangible assets to offer as collateral, chances of obtaining a loan from the bank become minimal. Debt financing in start-ups therefore happens in the form of venture debt. Venture debt is offered by registered non-banking financial corporations (NBFC) without taking any collateral. Since venture debt firms offer unsecured loans that have a higher risk, their interest rates are generally higher, usually averaging around 18 per cent annually, though they may go up to as high as 24 per cent.

Venture debt is typically preferred by founders to cover short-term expenses of a company. E-commerce and D2C start-ups, for instance, may look towards venture debt firms to fund short-term operational expenses related to working capital, or slightly longer duration requirements such as the expansion of offline stores. Both these purposes require upfront capital but there's usually a foreseeable timeframe within which they can be recovered through operational revenues.

It is important to point out here that venture debt firms do not prefer to invest in the early stages of a start-up. They favour the ones who have already found their product-market fit and have earned or raised enough capital to be able to repay their debt in case things go south. Sometimes, venture debt firms may also keep an option of converting their debt into equity at a later stage. If they find that the start-up is growing fast, they may want to benefit from the upside. They might therefore keep a clause in the agreement that gives them the option of converting a certain portion, usually 10–20 per cent, and in some rare cases, even 100 per cent of the debt into equity in the future.

b. **Equity Financing**

Equity financing implies that an investor invests money in a company in return for a stake in it. Angel investors, venture capital firms and private equity firms are known to invest in start-ups in this mode. Unlike debt funding, there is no assurance or obligation of a fixed return in equity financing. If the start-up fails, the investor may even lose the entire investment. On the other hand, if the start-up grows, so does the value of their investment. At an exit event (investment by a larger investor, IPO or acquisition), the investor can sell their stake in the business and potentially pocket a multifold return on the principal investment. Equity investors, therefore, make use of their conviction and analysis of start-ups to find the right opportunities that hold the most potential for success. At the same time, they also take protective measures, such as liquidation preference, to safeguard their interests.

Contrary to the general perception, equity is a more expensive source of capital than debt. As far as debt financing goes, once you repay the principal and the interest amount to the lender, the deal is over. The lender does not have any say, for instance, in how you run the business or what you do with the money. In equity financing, however, you give away part ownership of your company. The shareholder not only gets extraordinary returns in case of success but, in several cases, also some form of control over the business. It stands to reason then that a start-up founder may not wish to give away equity to fund short-term, operational expenses where returns are foreseeable. In such cases, it makes more sense to raise funds through debt.

What is also in use, is a hybrid form of financing—a mix of debt and equity mainly carried out through convertible securities. In this case, the investor puts money in a start-up as a loan (debt financing), and as the company grows, the invested amount is converted into shares (equity financing). We will be referring to convertible securities at several points in the book.

Stages of Equity Funding

Pre-Seed, Seed, Series A, B, C; odds are that you have heard of these terms in the context of start-up fundraising. These are simply the various stages/rounds in which start-ups tend to raise funds.

The table below lists the different rounds of funding and details what the possible objectives of each round are, as well as the investors involved in each of these stages.

Round	Investor	Objective
Pre-Seed	Friends and Family	1. Build a prototype of the product. 2. Refine the product. 3. Achieve Product–Market Fit.
Seed	Angel Investors and Micro VCs	1. Acquire the first paying users of the business. 2. Rapidly scale the number of users. 3. Build features and fixes that would help the business serve a high user base.
Series A	At least one marquee VC firm	The focus of the business shifts from scaling users to scaling revenue.
Series B	Marquee VC firms	1. The business will rapidly spend on marketing, branding and top-tier talent to hopefully become a well-known name in the market. 2. Might also make small acquisitions.

Round	Investor	Objective
Series C and beyond	Marquee VCs, Private Equity firms, Strategic Investors	1. The business cash flows and financial models are studied with tight scrutiny. 2. Valuations start rationalizing to multiples of profitability expectation rather than to multiples of revenue or users.

Apart from the stages shown above, start-ups may also raise money between two large rounds, like a pre-Series A or a pre-Series B. Known as bridge rounds, they help start-ups extend their runway to the next stage.

While we have discussed the investor types briefly in an earlier chapter, it will help to get into some more detail, this time in terms of the various kinds of funding rounds they support.

Pre-Seed Round

This typically is the idea stage of your start-up. Needless to say, there aren't many people backing you at this stage. The typical participants at this stage are your friends and family. In fact, the pre-seed round is also referred to as the F&F round in common parlance, the two Fs being friends and family, of course. I have, however, always referred to this round as the friends, family and fools round. Don't get me wrong—I do not wish to demean this important cohort that handholds you through the early stages of the start-up. The only reason I refer to them as fools is that they generally have little idea about how and if the business will take off, how the concept of valuation works, what is in it for them, etc. . . . yet they are more than keen to support you as they are emotionally invested in you. This is all the more reason why it is the moral responsibility of the founder to give these early investors an option to exit at the earliest. Their motivation to invest was just you, and prioritizing them is only fair.

Other than family and friends, some other early takers at the idea stage include incubators that are generally set up by trust funds in educational institutions. Some of the most popular incubators are run by the IITs, IIMs and other top colleges in the country and usually accommodate student founders. In addition, companies such as Google, Microsoft, Cisco, among others, have their own incubation centres where they support start-ups that align with their long-term strategy. Incubators typically select founders with promising start-up ideas and offer them office space to work out of, access to other early-stage investors and more. In return, they take some equity in start-ups that is usually defined per cohort in the different institutions. Incubators that have a large corpus, often donated by alumni or surplus funds, may also invest in these start-ups.

One other cohort that can step up and invest in your idea at the pre-seed stage are colleagues and alums of your existing company. McKinsey consultants and alums, for instance, run a fund colloquially called M Capital that is known to back ideas of McKinsey employees who quit the company to launch a start-up. Implied in the investment is the fact that the person who has made it to McKinsey and has worked there is smart enough to take a bet on a viable idea. Employees branching out from marquee organizations such as Hindustan Unilever, Flipkart, etc., have similarly found it easy to raise early funds. This, in fact, brings us to the importance of your network when you are turning to entrepreneurship. Whether it is your alma mater or the organizations that you have worked at, you can lean on your network for various aspects. On a related note, while it is fashionable to speak of start-up founders who are drop-outs, it stands to reason that it can be that much harder for them to find support in the absence of solid networks. Of course, there are exceptions, but they are typically few and far between.

Let's spend some time now understanding how investments at the pre-seed stage are made, especially since assessing the valuation of the start-up when you have only a germ of an idea isn't particularly easy. These investments typically make use of a convertible note, which we made a reference to, earlier. Let's take an example to understand how this works. Say your family is making an investment of Rs 20 lakh in your start-up at the pre-seed stage. What you could do is agree to take this money at an interest rate of 20 per cent per annum, with a proviso that if you happen to raise investment from an investor at a valuation of, say, Rs 5 crore, your family will be entitled to convert their loan and the interest due to equity at this valuation. Alternately, if you feel that 20 per cent is too steep an interest cost to pay, you can also choose to offer equity at a 20 per cent discount on the valuation you receive from the investor. In the example above, at a 20 per cent discount, the Rs 20 lakh gets converted at Rs 4 crore as opposed to Rs 5 crore, fetching your family an equity of 5 per cent in your venture. Interestingly, a discount of 20 per cent on the valuation with conversion of debt happening to equity within twelve months translates to over 25 per cent interest rate.

Seed Round

This round, meant typically to help you market your product and acquire the first large set of users, is led largely by angel investors. We have seen earlier that angel investors are essentially high-net-worth individuals with investments across asset classes.

Whether or not an angel investor will choose to invest in your business will depend a lot upon on their individual evaluation, beliefs, biases, preferences and principles. If you have watched episodes of *Shark Tank India*, you'd have noticed that different sharks (or angels) present different reasons for investing or rejecting a business, which essentially includes one or a mix of the following:

- Belief in the founder's profile and track record
- Belief in the founder's vision
- Recent performance of the start-up
- Expertise and interest in a particular domain (viewers of *Shark Tank* would recall Namita Thapar's line, '*Ye meri* expertise *nahi hai*. I am out,' that she often used to explain her non-participation in a particular deal and that also went on to spark a meme fest on social media)
- Positive outlook for a particular industry
- Attractive business model and scope to scale
- Support for a larger cause

It is important to remember that many angels can be highly industry-specific due to their experience in a particular field. If one is a stalwart of the healthcare industry, for instance, and is looking to invest Rs 50 lakh in start-ups, one may opt to invest Rs 5 lakh each across ten different health-tech start-ups. In looking for angel investors, it will help for you to keep their individual expertise in mind. The portfolio of companies invested in by an angel investor also gives a fair indication of their preferences. Founders can use this information to determine whether or not a particular angel may be interested in their start-up.

Some of the other aspects to keep in mind when pitching to angel investors include the fact that in current times, it has become a sort of status symbol to identify oneself as an angel investor. If you try to look for angel investors on a platform like LinkedIn, for instance, you will come across thousands of profiles stating that they invest in early-stage start-ups. While this may raise your hopes immediately, you may want to be cautiously optimistic, knowing that when it comes to actual disbursement of money from this cohort, it may not come so easily. Also, their cheque sizes are quite small, sometimes woefully so.

What could work in your favour, however, is to remember that this is one investor class that is completely driven by the fear of missing out (FOMO). Angel investors typically invest in groups. It will be worthwhile identifying the queen bee, as it were, for when she invests, the rest are likely to follow suit. If any of the sharks, for instance, were to invest in your start-up, others typically could follow suit. Many angels have also built small limited liability partnerships (LLPs) where they have created a pool of money. The angel responsible for sourcing a good deal typically charges a 'carry' fee from the other angels whenever there is a big exit. It will be worth reaching out to such groups. Angel syndicates are yet another important resource to reach out to. The Mumbai Angels Network at one time, for instance, was extremely popular and has recently been acquired by 360 ONE, formerly known as IIFL Wealth and Asset Management. Other popular syndicates include Hyderabad Angels Network, Chandigarh Angels Network, to name a couple.

Since time is an important currency and your energy is finite, it will also help for founders to keep an eye on whether or not an investor has invested in any business lately. No investments in the last twelve months, for instance, could indicate that they may have burnt their fingers somewhere and hence have taken a break on investments. It is advisable to target angels who have put money into start-ups in the past two months, for instance, as the success rate there is likely to be encouraging.

How Much to Raise in an Angel/Seed Round

In raising any round, it is important to identify the milestones you want to hit and then work backwards to calculate the expenses required to meet them and also keep some buffer for safety. In determining how much you should raise in a round, it is important to remember that typically, any round of investment should cover the runway for at least eighteen to twenty-four months. This is because closing a funding round in itself takes an average of nine months. If you are really lucky and the deal is very hot, you could get an early commitment. Even then, you need to add the time for due diligence, paperwork and more. If you haven't raised enough funds to last eighteen to twenty-four months, you could well be in a situation where even before one round is over, you need to get back to starting to raise capital.

Series A/B/C

While there is no clear definition of the nomenclature of funding rounds, typically, it is when you hit a certain monthly recurring revenue that a marquee VC firm, early PE firm or a family office comes in with institutional capital. This is what is referred to as Series A funding. This, in turn, is followed by Series B, C and so on. Each of these rounds have different objectives from the standpoint of the start-up, while the valuation principles also change with each round. As the table at the beginning of this segment delineates, at Series A, the chief focus of the start-up moves from scaling users to scaling revenue. At Series B, the business typically wants to invest in marketing, branding and more. By the time the start-up is raising a Series C round, the investor is looking for multiples of profitability as opposed to multiples of users or revenue.

VC Business Model

While a start-up is extremely focused on evolving its own business model (and rightly so), they will benefit greatly in the process of fundraising if they spent some time in understanding the business model of a VC.

The broad business model of a VC firm, of course, is to identify promising start-ups with potential for growth, invest in them in return for a stake in the company, and then sell their stake in whole or in parts to obtain a healthy return on their initial investments. So, while start-ups are absolutely focused on competing with each other to raise money from VCs, VCs, in turn, also compete with each other to find the best start-ups to fund.

Triple T

In the early stages of a start-up, some of the key metrics that help VCs assess the potential of a start-up can be categorized as what I like to call Triple T, namely, Team, TAM and Traction.

It is only fair that the credibility of the initial team of co-founders is the first aspect that should drive investors. After all, their money will ride on this team that needs to have both the vision and the executing capacity to drive the business. VCs therefore tend to back a competent founding team with complementary skills. In this regard, solid academic credentials will definitely stand you in good stead. Not without reason.

Look at the chart below and you will know why investors, for instance, are bullish on IIT graduates:

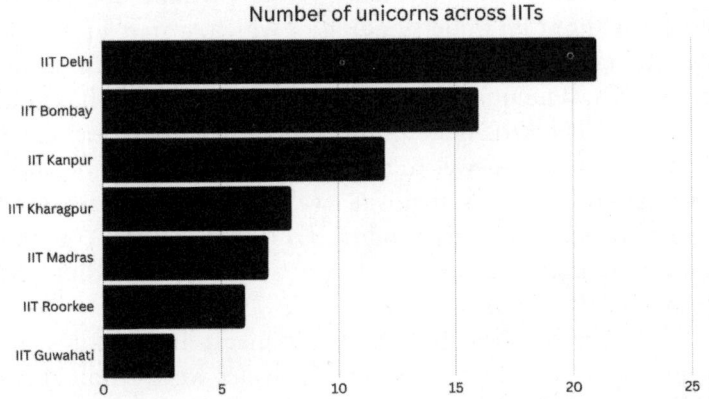

Source: News reports, numbers as of May 2022

Successful past exits similarly tend to tip the scales in your favour.

We have discussed the second T, namely the concept of TAM or the total addressable market, earlier in our discussion. A large TAM is crucial for attracting investors seeking high equity returns since it demonstrates a significant market opportunity and potential for substantial growth and revenue.

Last and definitely not least is the traction your product is showing in the market. Investors will look at whether or not you have indeed achieved product-market fit as seen through various metrics such as the Net Promoter Score, monthly recurring revenue and more. Gross margins and unit economics will be other focus areas for investors as they look for both current performance and the potential the business holds through future projections of revenues and profit.

What Kind of Financial Returns Does an Investor Look For?

At this point, it will be worthwhile to examine one critical aspect without an understanding of which, a start-up will at best be taking shots in the dark when trying to raise funds from VCs. The question that begs an answer is: What kind of financial returns does an investor actually look for? Only if you know the answer to this question and if your business plan demonstrates the requisite levels of returns, do you stand a fair chance of getting funded. To be able to arrive at this understanding, we need to begin with understanding the source of VC funds.

The funds that the VC firms invest in start-ups are generally pooled in from several high-net-worth individuals (HNIs) and institutions with a promise of giving them exceptional returns within a promised timeframe. Let us refer to the people from where VCs source funds as limited partners (LP). This is how the funds flow:

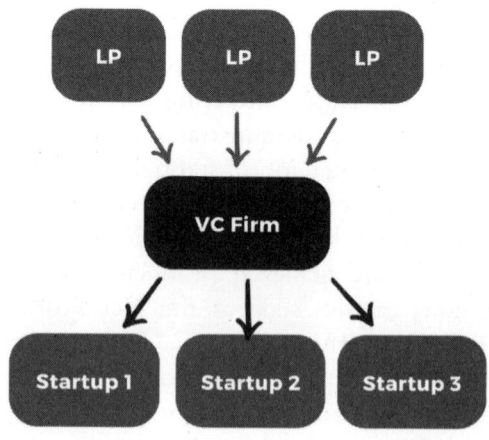

Needless to mention, the investors who are offering funds to the VC firms have a gamut of investable opportunities open to them. It is only if they can receive higher returns in start-up investments (which are implicitly risky), as opposed to the other models of investing available to them, that they will consider it an attractive investment proposition. From an entrepreneur's point of view, the aspect to note here is that you are competing not just with other start-ups but with all other investable opportunities, to be able to make the cut.

In this section, let us try to decode investor expectations by way of tangible numbers. Broadly, the financial returns expected by investors, and hence by the VC companies investing in your start-up, can be expressed by way of the following equation:

$$R_i = R_f + \beta_i \times (R_m - R_f)$$

- R_i is the expected return on the investment;
- R_f is the risk-free rate;
- β_i is the beta of the investment;
- R_m is the expected return of the market.

While the equation may seem intimidating at first glance, it isn't really so. Look at it like this: the expected return on start-up investments is a function of three elements: a) the risk-free rate of return that prevails in the market; b) the expected returns you can get from market investments; and c) the risk involved in the start-up proposition.

Before we go on to plot the actual values for each of these elements, let us understand how the risk/return relationship for different financial opportunities stacks up.

The diagram below shows a typical progression:

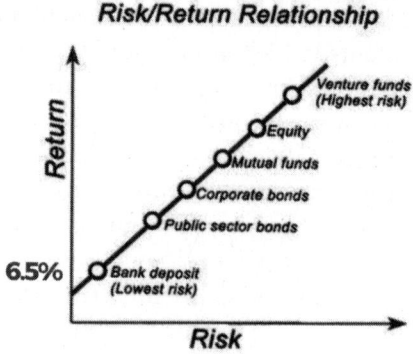

Clearly the risk and hence the returns are lowest for bank deposits, followed by public sector bonds, corporate bonds, mutual funds, equity and finally that of venture funds.

In the above equation, in order to begin with supplementing the value of risk-free return, let us consider the returns that banks typically make on their investments.

Comparison of Business Loan Interest Rates 2024

Bank/NBFCs	Interest Rate
Axis Bank	10.75% p.a. onwards
Bajaj Finserv	9.75% - 30% p.a.
Flexiloans	1% per month onwards
HDB Financial Services Ltd.	8% - 26% p.a.
HDFC Bank	10.75% - 25% p.a.
IDFC First Bank	10.50% p.a. onwards
Indifi	1.50% per month onwards
Kotak Mahindra Bank	16% - 26% p.a.
Lendingkart	12% - 27% p.a.
Mcapital	2% per month onwards
NeoGrowth Finance	15% - 40% p.a.
Tata Capital	12% p.a. onwards

Assuming that banks lend at 16 per cent and borrow at 8 per cent, and also lose an average of 1.5 per cent to non-performing assets (NPA), it pegs its return at an average of 6.5 per cent.

Similarly, individuals make returns on bank deposits at close to 6–7 per cent p.a., which could be called a risk-free rate of return for the sake of simplicity.

That established, let us move on now to the next variable, namely the expected rate of return from the market, for which let us consider the returns earned by mutual funds as also by the NIFTY 50. Here is how that data would stack up as in July 2024.

I've picked this time for reference as this is when the equity markets had been performing fabulously for a period of three years, and more so in the previous twelve months.

And how the stock markets perform at any time greatly determines how investors feel about other types of private investments in businesses as well.

	5Y	3Y
Bandhan Nifty 50 Index Fund Direct Plan Growth	▲ 15.95%	▲ 15.24%
HSBC Nifty 50 Index Fund Direct Growth	--	▲ 15.16%
Motilal Oswal Nifty 50 Index Fund Direct Growth	--	▲ 15.15%
UTI Nifty 50 Index Fund-Growth Option- Direct	▲ 15.76%	▲ 15.15%
SBI Nifty Index Fund Direct Growth	▲ 15.59%	▲ 15.14%
DSP Nifty 50 Index Fund Direct Growth	▲ 15.61%	▲ 15.14%
Tata Nifty 50 Index Fund Direct Plan	▲ 15.71%	▲ 15.14%
ICICI Prudential Nifty 50 Index Plan Direct Growth	▲ 15.75%	▲ 15.13%

#	Company Name	EV/EBITDA	5Y Sales Gr.(%)	5Y Profit Gr.(%)
1	LTIMindtree Ltd ★★★★☆	20.87	30.33	14.02
2	Bajaj Finance Ltd ★★★★★	14.35	26.49	34.41
3	ICICI Bank Ltd ★★★☆☆	14.47	21.96	34.08
4	Bajaj Finserv Ltd ★★★★☆	8.72	20.09	19.33
5	Titan Company Ltd ★★★☆☆	59.33	19.63	23.28
6	Adani Ports and Special Economic Zone Ltd ★★★★☆	20.14	19.58	12.76
7	IndusInd Bank Ltd ★★★★★	7.84	18.60	9.65
8	Axis Bank Ltd ★★★★☆	13.15	18.19	96.23
9	Shriram Finance Ltd ★★★☆☆	7.49	17.74	7.96
10	Kotak Mahindra Bank Ltd ★★★★★	17.63	17.72	20.68

With returns from mutual funds pegged at an average of 15.7 per cent p.a. and equity at an average of 25 per cent in the previous twelve months, let us consider that the average expected return of the market was broadly in the region of 18 per cent at the time of this analysis in July 2024.

In supplementing these figures in the above equation, this is how the equation would pan out:

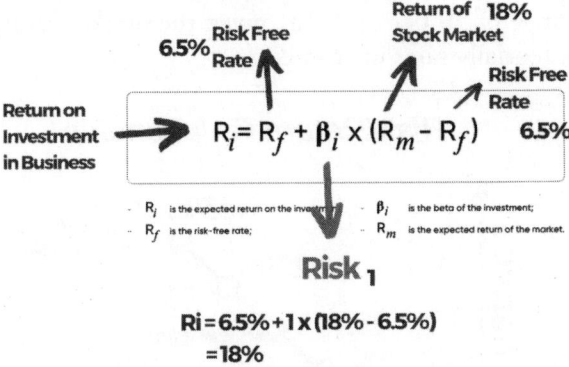

$$R_i = 6.5\% + 1 \times (18\% - 6.5\%)$$
$$= 18\%$$

There you go. By substituting the numbers above, you reach a figure of 18 per cent, as an expected rate of return on investment. The risk of investing in a start-up, however, is definitely higher than investing in India's top listed companies, for instance, which in itself offers an 18 per cent return, as we saw earlier. We therefore need to do one last thing and that is substitute the risk or Beta in the above equation from 1 to at least 1.5. In which case, the numbers will change as below:

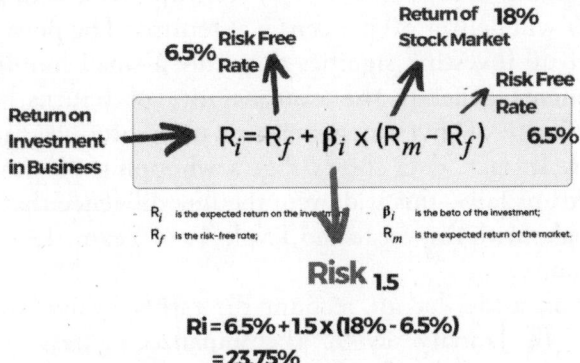

$$R_i = 6.5\% + 1.5 \times (18\% - 6.5\%)$$
$$= 23.75\%$$

The rate of return now mathematically jumps up to around 25 per cent p.a. For their risky start-up investments to make sense, the on-ground expected returns, in fact, tend to hover in the range of 30 per cent p.a., given the market returns on other potentially safer instruments.

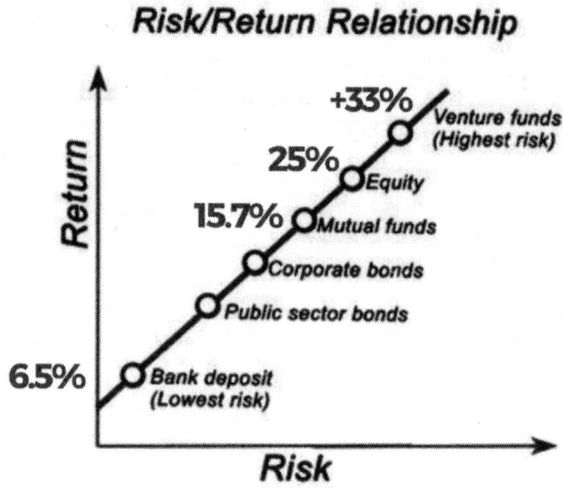

There is yet another aspect that deserves a fair understanding at this point. Which is, not every start-up investment made by VCs will deliver 30 per cent p.a. returns. The power law of start-up investing signifies that only a small number of investments generate the vast majority of returns, while the majority of investments either fail or produce modest returns. In fact, data shows that a whopping 90 per cent of start-ups fail—this is despite the due diligence that VCs may make with respect to the Triple Ts of Team, TAM and Traction.

As an aside, let me recount the rather funny story of Raven. In January 1999, a chimpanzee actress named Raven (the star of *Babe: Pig in the City*) threw ten darts at a dartboard of 133 Internet-related companies. Within six trading days, one of her picks was up a whopping 95 per cent! By the year's end, Raven's portfolio of ten randomly selected stocks had outperformed over 6000 Internet and technology money managers, earning an astonishing 213 per cent return. 'Chimp '99 Champ! Makes Monkey of Wall Street,' read the headline on Market Watch (source: www.prosperitythinkers.com). The veracity of the story apart, the fact remains that even the most prudent diligence cannot predict success with 100 per cent accuracy, either at the stock market or in the start-up space. The element of luck definitely plays an important part. But we digress.

Getting back to our discussion, let us for a minute assume that a VC has raised Rs 100 crore from LPs with a promise to return funds and profit thereof in eight years. Of the Rs 100 crore raised, the VC will charge a management fee @ 2 per cent p.a. to run their operations, amounting, in this case, to Rs 16 crore over a period of eight years. The investable funds available to the VC are therefore 100-16 = Rs 84 crore. To minimize their risk, VCs tend to invest across various start-ups. Let us assume that they decide to spread this money over twenty start-ups. The investment per start-up therefore amounts to 84/20 = Rs 4.2 crore per start-up. Given a failure rate of 90 per cent, of the twenty start-ups that the VC invests in, only two have the probability to succeed. The amount invested in these two start-ups is a cumulative of Rs 8.4 crore.

Let us also assume that the time taken by VCs to find worthy start-ups to invest in averages two years. Since the VC has to make its deliveries to the LP in eight years, what that means is effectively it has six years to exit these start-ups profitably. Now consider this, even if the two start-ups had to return just the principal amount to the LPs in the six years remaining, what return would they have to give per annum?

This is how the math will add up:

Initial Value	84 ₹
Final Value Costs	1000 ₹
Duration of Investment	6 Yrs
CAGR	51.11%

Figures in million

That is a 12x return (1000/84) in six years each, just to return the fund to LPs with 0 per cent interest p.a. No LP would be happy with that, of course. As another experiment, even if the two successful start-ups had to return 2x the principal amount of the fund, any guesses on what return they would have to give per annum?

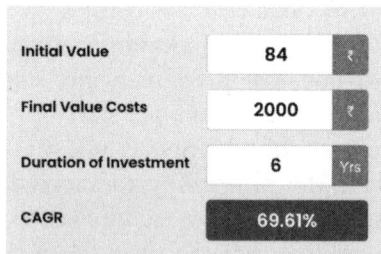

That's a 24X Return in 6 years each just to return the Fund to LPs with ~12% p.a.

Figures in million

Whether LPs would be happy with a 9–12 per cent p.a. return after taking such a high risk on their money is anybody's guess. As seen from our earlier discussion on the expected rate of return, the absolute minimum rate that an LP would expect would be no less than 25 per cent.

The Minimum Return LPs would expect would be no lesser than 25% p.a.

Initial Value	1000 ₹
Final Value Costs	4000 ₹
Duration of Investment	6 Yrs
CAGR	25.99%

Figures in million

To be able to achieve a 25 per cent overall return, the two successful start-ups will need to deliver as much as a 90 per cent p.a. return each for six years. See for yourself:

That's a 90% p.a. Return by the 2 Startups each for 6 years!

Initial Value	84 ₹
Final Value Costs	4000 ₹
Duration of Investment	6 Yrs
CAGR	90.38%

Figures in million

In short, if you cannot deliver a 90 per cent-odd rate of return consistently year-on-year for six years (which can be simply thought of as doubling every year for six years), you may be a great business, but you may still not be VC-investable.

The idea of presenting you with all the above data isn't to discourage you from seeking funding but to lay the broad canvas in front of you realistically, for you to be adequately prepared for what is to come.

How to Value Your Business

Having discussed some basics of VC funding and their expectations, it is time to segue into a topic that is often a bone of contention between entrepreneurs and investors. On the one hand, entrepreneurs need to put a value on their start-up in order to raise money; on the other, investors need to put a value on their investments to ensure an adequate return on investment. Often times, the two could have diametrically opposite views on what the start-up is worth and how much equity the investor should receive in exchange for his capital.

Let us discuss the basic concept of valuation first, over a cup of coffee.

The Worth of a Cup of Coffee

I often visit the Blue Tokai outlet in the market close to my home and order a cup of Iced Americano. The last time I visited, I paid Rs 350 for it. However, would everyone be happy to pay Rs 350 for a cup of coffee? Not if you consider the fact that coffee is consumed by different consumers for different reasons. If, for instance, you are looking at receiving your morning caffeine hit, you would be perfectly happy with your homemade coffee. Someone else may relish the coffee available at a roadside stall for Rs 20. Yet others would love to work out of a coffee shop and be happy to pay Rs 350 as they work in comfort all day. For someone else, the allure of a coffee shop may well be that it offers the opportunity for Instagrammable pictures. Clearly, it is the value that they derive from their experience that justifies their spending on more or less the same beverage—one that is brewed from roasted and ground seeds of the tropical evergreen coffee plant, anyway. While the basic ingredients are the same, what is different for different consumers is the perceived value. It is this perceived value that, in turn, justifies the price that the consumer is willing to pay.

So it is with start-ups. It is the perceived value of the start-up in the eyes of the investor that determines its valuation. Let us take an example from the start-up world to be able to understand this aspect better. What would you say is this company's business model?

What's this Company's Business Model?

I am guessing most of you having identified it as Uber, would respond stating it connects travellers to rides. When I further ask people who this company's competitors are, the common response that I get is the names of other players in the ride-hailing space.

Now, supposing Uber was to add another option to their offerings? Something like this:

Do you Notice anything Different?

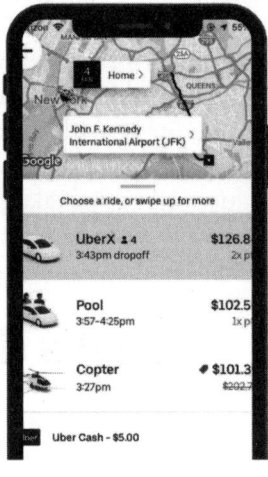

Clearly, by that one addition of a helicopter to its offerings, the company's value proposition would change significantly as would its competitors. It would also change its valuation, wouldn't you agree?

As they say, for an understanding of the future, you need to look to the past. As a matter of fact, the valuation for Uber did change in the past with a simple change in perspective. Dr Aswath Damodaran, a professor of finance at the New York University's Stern School of Business, is a globally renowned expert on valuation. Using a conventional approach in 2014, he had initially valued Uber at $6 billion with the narrative of the company being a cab aggregator for the US. The next year though, he went on to revalue the company at around $23 billion. The increase in valuation stemmed from the perspective that Uber would emerge as a logistics provider for the whole world. Notably, Uber hadn't actually expanded to too many other countries by then, but there was this notion that the company had the potential to expand geographically as well as functionally. You can see in the above example how a simple change in perspective resulted in nearly a four-time increase in valuation.

Factors Impacting Valuation

Traditionally, the concept of valuation was applicable only to profitable businesses. It came into play when a business was being acquired by another or when it decided to go public by way of an initial public offering (IPO). The quantum of speculation in determining valuation was also relatively low since the parameters involved in determining valuation broadly included the tangible cashflow generated by the business, the assets it owned and so forth.

The rise of the Internet, with its immense possibilities, however, changed it all. The fundamental change that the Internet brought about was the ease of discoverability of businesses and their expansion possibility. Businesses could now scale that much faster. The potential for such businesses to rake in super-normal revenues thus became incredibly high. In a scenario such as this, valuing a business basis its current profits began to seem increasingly unfair. In fact, future profitability evolved as a better representation for a business than its present performance.

Let us try to understand it by way of an example. Products of companies such as Google, Facebook and Amazon, for instance, are used by virtually everyone in the world with access to the Internet. These companies were therefore able to create a near monopoly in their industries. Once they gained access to a large number of customers with their first core offering, they also built other products that they were able to successfully cross-sell. Needless to say, the perspective of investors on companies that could create such monopolies resulted in seemingly high valuations.

Come to think of it, investor valuations tend to go up when a start-up displays one or more of the following three characteristics in their bid to disrupt a new market or industry:

- First mover: the first to disrupt a market
- Fastest: gaining market share most rapidly
- Most efficient: incurring the least costs and generating incredible returns

The other factors that impact valuation include:

Stage of the Start-Up

Valuations differ at different stages of the start-up based primarily on what a start-up has on offer. At the pre-seed stage, the start-up only has an idea and commands a certain valuation, as opposed to the seed stage when it also has a Minimum Viable Product. At the Series A stage, it also has a product; at Series B, it is showing early growth; at Series C, it is scaling and so on. It is only fair that the valuation it commands at each of these stages is different. Below is a handy infographic with broad industry averages that encapsulates this concept:

STRUiC STARTUP SAVANT	Pre-seed	Seed	Series A	Series B	Series C
Capital Raised	$5-250k	$2.2M (average)	$15.6M (average)	$33M (average)	$59M (average)
Investors	Family & Friends, Angels	F&F, Angels, Accelerator, VC, PE	VC, PE	VC, PE	VC, PE
What You Have	Idea	MVP	Product	Early Growth	Scale
Working Toward	Proof of Concept or Prototype	Validation	Traction	Scale	Exit

Industry and Business Model

Valuations also tend to differ based on the industry you operate in and the business model you have. Tech start-ups, for example, often have high valuations due to their scalability and market potential. Similarly, industries with high demand or emerging trends (like clean energy or AI) may see inflated valuations compared to traditional sectors. In terms of business models, companies with recurring revenue models (like SaaS or subscription-based businesses) often secure higher valuations due to predictable income. Businesses with asset-light models may command higher multiples too.

Not just valuation, the funding your company receives is also a function of the industry, with some industries being more popular than others. Below is a quick indicative trend of how investment levels across industries are increasing or declining over the years:

Changing landscape of startup investment

Percent of total startup investment going to broad industries by year | Jan 2019 – June 2023

Industry Broad	2019	2020	2021	2022	2023	
SaaS	42%	33%	38%	36%	30%	↓
Pharma/Biotech	8%	15%	11%	12%	15%	↑
Healthtech	12%	15%	12%	12%	12%	—
Energy	2%	1%	3%	5%	11%	↑
Hardware	6%	4%	5%	7%	10%	↑
Consumer	14%	12%	12%	10%	8%	↓
Fintech	11%	12%	13%	11%	5%	↓
Medical Devices	3%	3%	2%	2%	4%	—
Education	1%	2%	1%	1%	2%	—
Advertising Tech	1%	1%	1%	1%	1%	—
Gaming	2%	1%	1%	2%	1%	—

While several of the factors we saw above impact valuation, what is also important to recognize is that with the nature of assets becoming intangible and the business environment more dynamic, valuing a start-up today often involves a high level of speculation. With several variables, value, much like beauty, tends to lie in the eye of the beholder. So much so that if two experts are left to value the same company, odds are that their numbers won't match.

That said, let us look at some broad methods by which investors approach valuation.

Valuation Methods

There are several methods to value companies, which are widely in use. We will look at some of them in the pages to follow. If you are keen on getting into the subject of valuation in depth, I would strongly recommend reading Dr Aswath Damodaran's books—remember we made a reference to his valuations in the context of Uber earlier?

Discounted Cash Flows (DCF)

The DCF method is perhaps the most accepted way to compute valuations of profitable businesses. Simply put, this approach takes into account the current performance of the business in terms of net cash inflows while assumptions are made on its ability to generate future cash flows. The present value of expected future cash flows is then found out using a discounted rate.

Essentially what investors are trying to do in this method is to use the present value of money to determine whether the future cash flows are greater than the value of the initial investment. In sum, you are using discounted cash flow analysis to estimate the money an investor might receive from an investment, adjusted for the time value of money.

Here's broadly how the DCF method works:

$$DCF = \frac{CF_1}{(1+r)^1} + \frac{CF_2}{(1+r)^2} + \frac{CF_n}{(1+r)^n}$$

CF_1 = The cash flow for year one
CF_2 = The cash flow for year two
CF_n = The cash flow for additional years
r = The discount rate

Let's take two examples to understand this. One where the cash flow is the same in each period and one where it differs in different years:

	B	C	D	E	F	G	H
1							
2	When cash flows are the same in each period						
3	Cash flows	1,000.0					
4	t (periods)	5					
5	r (discount rate)	25%					
6	Present value	2,689.3	=-(PV(C5,C4,C3))				
7							
8	When cash flows are not the same in each period						
9	Period (t)		1	2	3	4	5
10	Cash flows		1,000.0	1,245.0	1,258.0	1,568.0	1,895.0
11	Discount rate (r)		25%	25%	25%	25%	25%
12	Present value		800.0	796.8	644.1	642.3	621.0
13							
14	Sum of present values	3,504.1					

In the above examples, you will see how the valuation is arrived at, factoring in the current values of future cashflows. Now if you had to keep the return from investment constant at 25 per cent, what are the two factors you can change to increase valuation? Clearly, they are:

1) Operating Cash Flows
2) Future Growth Rate

The DCF method is considered to offer a more comprehensive valuation than other methods since it considers all expected future cash flows. However, it is important to note that the DCF method is only used for mature companies that are close to profitability and not for early stage start-ups.

The DCF method is best used for companies that may be nearing their IPO or a public listing, which is why I prefer to just mention it here and not dive deeper into explaining it in depth for the purpose of this book.

Transaction Comparables Method

With early-stage start-ups contending with a lot of uncertainty, determining cash flows with accuracy isn't the easiest task. The transactions comparable method, therefore, uses proxies or substitutes of metrics for the valuation of a company. Simply put, it compares a start-up to its closest competitor and ascertains a valuation primarily considering the multiples achieved by these companies. Based on this analysis, a suitable multiple is used to arrive at the company's valuation.

Let us take an example:

Fintech Transaction Comparables				
Particulars	Competing Startups			
Basics	**Gold Setu**	**Rupeek**	**Ruptok**	**Simpl**
Founded	2021	2015	2020	2015
Total Amount Raised	$ 2.39 Mn	$ 144 Mn	$ 3.54 Mn	$ 83 Mn
Website	goldsetu.co	rupeek.com	ruptok.com	getsimpl.com
First Round				
Period	Jun-21	Nov-15	Jan-21	Jun-15
Total Amount Raised	$ 1.19 Mn	$ 88.7k	$ 1.41 Mn	$ 1.3 Mn
Valuation	$ 5.12 Mn	$ 946k	$ 4.93 Mn	$ 6.06 Mn
Dilution	23.2%	9.4%	28.6%	21.5%
Second Round				
Period	Feb-22	Jun-16	Oct-21	Nov-16
Total Amount Raised	$ 1.2 Mn	$ 346k	$ 2.13 Mn	$ 1.27 Mn
Valuation	N/A	N/A	$ 25.2 Mn	$ 7.36 Mn
Dilution	N/A	N/A	8.5%	17.3%

In this example, I used the transaction comparables model to determine the valuation of a client who had built an online marketplace for jewellery and was looking to raise their first round of funding. We found that in the first round of investment, the four closest competitors raised an average investment of $1.2 million. The valuations of these companies lay at $5 million. Based on these numbers, raising a round of $1 million at a valuation of $5 million seemed to be a possibility. It was likely that the company would need to dilute 20 per cent stake if the investment went through.

Let me sound a word of caution here though—this is only a demonstrative example and the real investment raised will depend on a number of factors, including but not limited to the company's objectives, the milestones they hit over the next twelve to eighteen months and so on. Just because their competitors have raised a certain funding does not automatically make the company eligible for the same ask. What the method does achieve, however, is offering proxies that investors are comfortable with.

Trading Comparables Method

While the transactions comparable method seems to be a reasonable way to arrive at proxies, what needs to be kept in mind is that financial data of competitors isn't always easily available. In such cases, we turn to listed public companies that are legally bound to publish their data.

If you are keen to study an example where a trading comparable method has been used effectively, I would like to point you to the blog post of Alexander Jarvis, a UK-based investment banker titled 'How do you value your social media start-up with investors?' Even though the blog was written in 2017–18 and the data may seem outdated, the principles still hold. To sum up, Jarvis valued a fictitious social media platform called Awesome which had 5 million monthly active users (MAU), on the basis of this method. He went on to list as many as thirteen social media companies that went public or were merged or acquired. He also collected information on their market cap, and the MAU at the time of their IPO or acquisition. Then he calculated the value per user for each of the companies by dividing the valuation by the MAU count. For both Value/MAU and Valuation, he mentioned the minimum, the maximum and the mean and median values across these thirteen platforms, allowing him to arrive at a valuation range for Awesome. At this point, of course, Awesome's founders need to determine if they think they fall closer to the lower end of the spectrum or the higher end.

To use the trading comparables method effectively, one must thoroughly analyse the platforms being compared and identify why some achieved higher valuation than others. Also, since listed companies would be far advanced in their journeys, the use of judgement to break down the metrics objectively and draw meaningful comparisons is key.

Scorecard Method

The scorecard method isn't so much a method of arriving at a valuation but more an insight into how VCs evaluate potential start-ups. To understand the method, we need to know that different VCs have different thesis and investment philosophies. The scorecard method takes into account the 'thesis'—namely, a set of guiding principles or parameters that the VC considers before investing in a start-up. The VC under question develops a scorecard to rate different start-ups against these identified parameters.

Let us take an example:

Parameter	Total weight	Start-up 1	Start-up 2	Start-up 3
TAM	20	18	14	10
Industry	15	12	11	12
# Users	15	10	14	12
# Paying users	15	10	12	10
CAC	10	8	9	5

Parameter	Total weight	Start-up 1	Start-up 2	Start-up 3
ARR	10	5	6	4
MoM user growth	10	6	8	9
Churn	5	4	3	5
Total	**100**	**73**	**77**	**67**

TAM = Total Addressable Market
CAC = Customer Acquisition Cost
ARR = Annual Recurring Revenue (Rs)
MoM = Month on Month

The above, is of course a simplified example, but if for the purpose of understanding, we went by it, the VC firm would pick Start-up 2 to put their money on, as it scores the highest on their scorecard. The lower the score of a particular start-up against the parameters set by the VC, the higher the risk and hence the lower their valuation.

The actionable insight from the above method, for an entrepreneur, is that they need to evaluate the VC's portfolio of investments on the set parameters and see if they tend to fit in.

Actionable Insights for Entrepreneurs

Valuation, as you must have understood by now, is not plain fact-based mathematics. Since many assumptions about future performance are involved, the final number really depends on who is evaluating the company and what perspectives are being considered. Each of these methods also works best within a certain set of scenarios and no single method can be said to be universally correct.

A founder should ideally get their valuation computed internally with all the possible methods known. That would give them a wide range of valuation figures, and they'd know exactly which one serves them most favourably. Understanding the factors behind those methods would also help them be prepared with the right information on what potentially drives their valuation down and what can increase it. This knowledge can be used to negotiate a higher valuation with investors.

The methods that we discussed above, of course, apply only to unlisted private companies. They act as tools for investors to price the company when there is no clear, large-scale market consensus. Needless to say, all of this changes post-IPO, when the stock market decides the valuation on any given day. For a listed company, valuation on any given day can be arrived at simply by multiplying the share price with the total number of shares that constitute the company.

Valuation and Revenue Expectation

Having discussed several methods of valuation, let us also ask ourselves an important question, namely, having received a certain valuation, what kind of revenues would you be expected to deliver? Try and ascertain the revenues in the hypothetical situation below:

Say you have received a valuation of Rs 100 crore, when your revenue is Rs 10 crore. What should your revenue be on exit after five years for a 20x return to your investors?

To begin with, let us look at the revenue multiple being offered today. It is clearly 10x (100/10). Since the valuation expected is 20x after five years, it is 20*100 = Rs 2000 crore.

Now, what should the revenue be after five years for the company to be worth Rs 2000 crore? Clearly, it is Rs 200 crore (2000/10) while maintaining the 10x revenue multiple.

While this is a hypothetical example, you may be interested in looking at some industry-wide actual multiples in India and calculate the revenues required.

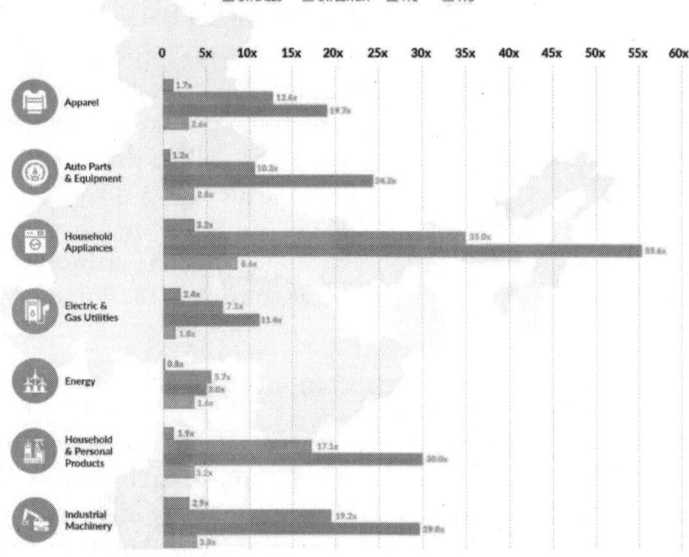

Industry Multiples In India

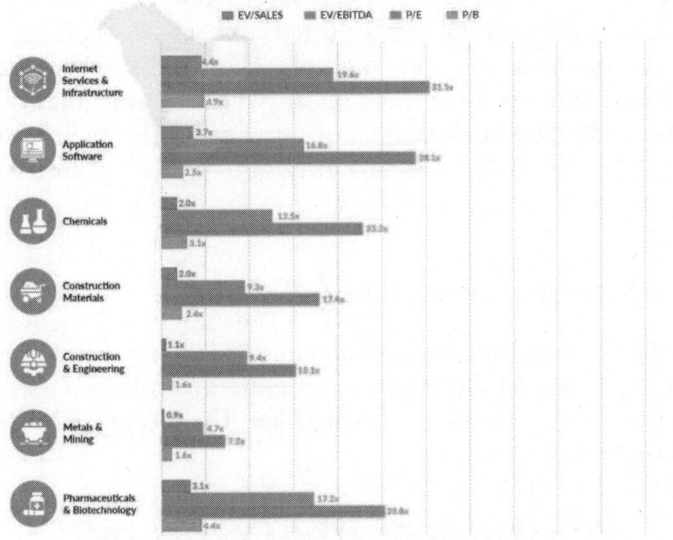

Industry Multiples In India

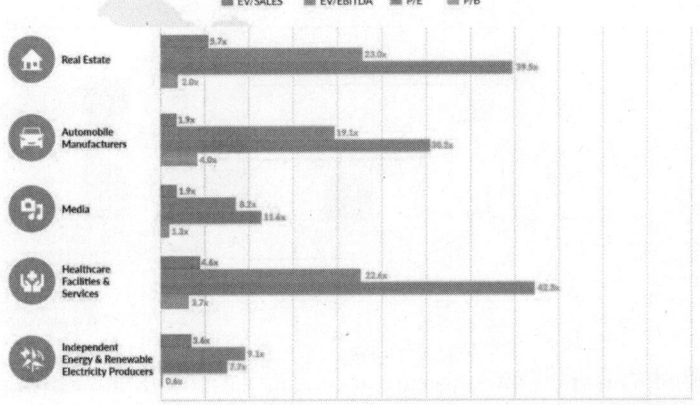

mintgenie

It shows you that a 10x revenue multiple is almost unheard of when a business matures and inches towards becoming profitable and closer to being a listed company.

A reasonable revenue multiple may be 3x when the business matures over five years, which means that to obtain a Rs 2000-crore valuation, it would need an annual revenue of Rs 2000/3 = Rs 667 crore and not Rs 200 crore as calculated above.

High Valuation versus Valuation Inflation

It will be interesting to look at some individual companies that have shown astronomical revenue growths and have achieved high valuations. Try and see if you can guess the names of these companies:

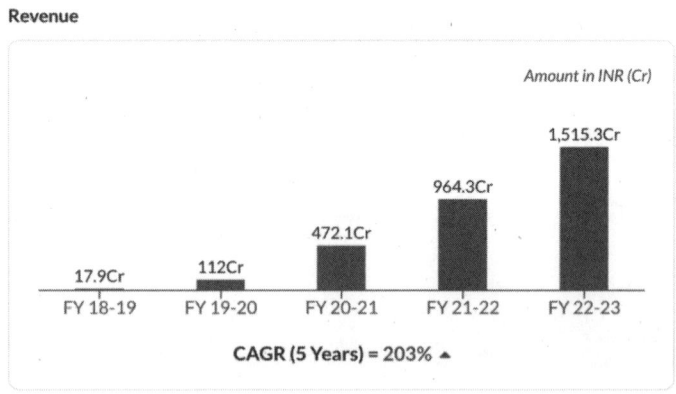

Well, it is the D2C skincare and beauty brand, Mamaearth.
Let us take one more shot.

Can you guess the Company?

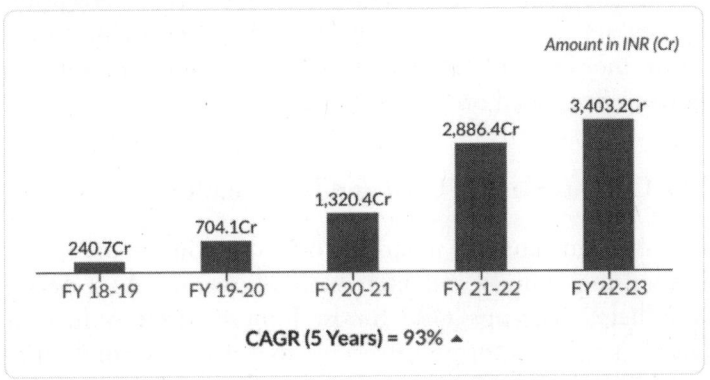

This time it is the digital-first consumer products company, boAt.

While the above companies have shown astronomical revenue growths that, in turn, have led to high valuations, in recent times we have also witnessed cases where a start-up receives an abnormally high valuation without a strong-enough performance to back it. Referred to as valuation inflation, this phenomenon tends to benefit early investors the most as it swells up the price of the shares that they hold and gives them a chance to make a hefty return on their investment.

Valuation inflation typically occurs while leading up to one of these two events—IPO or acquisition. While it may not always be the case, it is possible for existing investors and founders to hire PR firms to oversell growth prospects and create a false sense of expectation. Alternately, when offering the start-up for sale to a larger company, the valuation may be inflated. This inflation can occur in the form of the funding round itself wherein investors may put in a certain, probably smaller amount at a valuation significantly higher than in the previous funding round. This allows them to continue selling the growth story and create a positive perception. If they successfully find a buyer who agrees to their price point, they end up making a profit from an underperforming start-up just based on perceptions.

The Curious Case of Cred and Its Valuation

Kunal Shah-founded Cred is often in the news for its fundraising rounds and ultra-high valuations. As a person who helps start-ups raise funds, I must admit, valuations and business performance aside, that Kunal's fundraising capability is second to none. It also reflects the fact that he's probably different and more insightful than other founders, and VCs, who themselves constitute of extremely smart individuals, are willing to bet big on him and his start-up despite the noise around.

At first look, the valuation of Cred does not make sense. In June 2022, it was reported that they raised their latest funding at a valuation of a whopping $6.4 billion. In the financial year ending 2022, their revenues stood at Rs 95.5 crore, or roughly $12 million. Their consolidated losses were at Rs 523.8 crore, or roughly $68 million.

Their valuation, up until this point, is 533x their revenues! The 10–12x multiple that tech start-ups usually command is comfortably dwarfed by this figure. Why is Cred valued so highly by investors?

The reason, I feel, is the narrative about how the company plans to utilize the users on its platform. This information is not publicly available. But it surely is discussed between the founder and the investors.

Cred is building a community of credit-worthy individuals. This essentially means that these are people with a higher paying capacity and are less likely to default on payments than the average Indian. They have the capability to make high-value purchases and are a sound target group for anyone selling luxury or convenience. Cred offers such people incentives to stay and transact on their platform, collects their purchase data and is technically well poised to offer products or services that affluent individuals will happily pay for.

This data puts them in a position to offer several things, which they are. They are now a discovery platform for niche, luxury items. They also have a peer-to-peer lending platform. They have CRED pay, which allows you to make online payments seamlessly. And there's certainly a lot more brewing that we don't know about. With these offerings, they are also increasing the frequency of use of their customers as well as ramping up the number of loyal active users. While other products may have millions of users, the ones using Cred have a much higher paying capacity. If they continue to serve them well, the LTV of each such user can be potentially extremely high. And if there are millions of such customers, the valuation would somehow start making sense.

But this is what investors believe will happen in the future. Today, the criticism Cred receives is on its inability so far to generate the revenues expected from an entity priced so high.

I wish I had more information to give a more informed verdict. Only time will tell how the Cred story unfolds. Most people who offer commentary on its valuation do so with incomplete information. Without a complete background of the facts, one can only draw conjectures and not conclusions.

Is their valuation too high? It depends on the eye of the beholder.

* * *

How should founders think about valuation?

As we are getting to a close on this segment on valuation, we have two more aspects to cover: 1) How should founders think about valuation; and 2) How should founders decide how much equity to dilute in each round. Let us get to both these aspects.

The precedent to the question on how founders should think about valuation should actually be, 'Why are you starting up?' The purpose of becoming an entrepreneur varies with every individual as we have discussed earlier, and there is nothing right or wrong about it. Some do it for money, a few for impact and others to simply follow a passion. For someone looking to make money fast, chasing a high valuation and making a successful exit would be key. How effective this approach would be, though, is something I'm not sure about.

Since this question is more personal opinion than giving an absolute right answer, my three broad suggestions to founders would be:

1. Prioritize value over valuation
2. Build to last
3. Optimize growth, but rationally

Consider these suggestions after knowing that I'm an old-school romantic when it comes to businesses. I believe businesses should be built to last till perpetuity and not simply as an object to flip for a quick buck. I know there are many who would disagree with me and I respect that.

Let me briefly explain my three suggestions for founders below:

Prioritize Value over Valuation

It's hard to escape the valuation talk as a start-up founder today, especially for the ones who are dependent on VC funds to grow and sustain. But one should remember that valuation is derived from the value you add to your users' lives. When you stop adding value, they will move away and so will the valuation.

As a founder, it's imperative that you keep doing things that add tremendous value to your users. And question everything that doesn't. Everything that adds value is essential, everything else is noise. Stay away from the noise.

Build to Last

Companies become truly great when they're able to add value in a sustainable manner over a long period. HDFC, HUL, ITC, Marico, Axis Bank and Asian Paints are great examples in the Indian context. They have delivered consistent returns to their shareholders for decades only because they could grow sustainably. Today, we don't often measure them by their valuations.

One thing common among all these companies is their incredible business fundamentals. They are all pre-VC era companies, so obviously their manner and timelines of growth have been vastly different from what start-ups today experience.

In my opinion, every start-up must always have an eye on the traditional, core fundamentals of the business and not just the ones associated with valuation. Even though they may not perform optimally on such metrics, tracking them would ensure they don't become irreconcilable in the future. It then gives the start-up a greater chance to succeed over the long term, and really build to last.

Optimize Growth, but Rationally

Growth is important for any company. But what separates the great from the average ones is that they draw the line between growth and growth at all costs. Many VC-funded start-ups have, over the years, fallen into the spiral of growing unsustainably by burning inordinate amounts of cash, only to see their customers leaving when freebies stopped.

As a start-up founder today, whether you're VC-funded or not, you must always have the conviction to discourage anything that advocates irrational growth. One common symptom of such growth is an unusually high CAC. And this symptom often arises when start-ups raise a lot more money than they need and then proceed to splurge the surplus cash on highly ineffective activities. Bootstrapped companies never get this luxury, so they're forced to grow within their limited means, which often serves them well in the long run.

You, as the founder, must know how much is too much. There's no shame in raising a smaller round if it serves your purpose. It may mean that, sometimes, you would have to sacrifice valuation for sustainability. But if I were your adviser, I'd always encourage that approach.

Equity Dilution

That said, let us now address the question on how much equity should an entrepreneur dilute with each funding round. While dilution is a prerogative of the founder and depends a lot on what individual founder objectives are, it will be worthwhile to look at overall industry data to arrive at some averages.

In fact, let us begin this journey backwards and look at what percentage of their company do founders typically hold at IPO. Data shows that at the top SaaS companies, founder-CEOs own an average of 15 per cent of their company at IPO.

Ownership at IPO, pre-offering

	Founder 1	Founder 2	Founder 3	Ratio of F2/F1:
Klaviyo	38.10%	13.90%		36%
Atlassian	37.70%	37.70%		100%
ZoomInfo	32.10%	24.50%		76%
Zscaler	28.30%	solo		
New Relic	27.30%	solo		
Dropbox	24.40%	9.90%		41%
UiPath	25.60%	<5%		
Zoom	22.00%	solo		
GitLab	19.00%	<5%		
Appfolio	18.00%	7.30%		41%
Cloudflare	16.60%	5.60%	1.10%	34%
Fastly	15.60%	solo		
Monday	15.30%	5.60%		37%
Elastic	15.00%	solo		
Shopify	14.62%	2.49%		17%
Datadog	14.10%	8.90%		63%
Veeva	13.50%	3.10%		23%
Pluralsight	13.40%		1.60%	
Confluent	12.60%	6.90%	<5%	55%
Twilio	11.90%	<5%	<5%	
Hashicorp	11.50%	9.20%		80%
Crowdstrike	10.50%	<5%	<5%	
Okta	10.30%	6.20%		60%
Smartsheet	8.90%	2.30%		26%
HubSpot	8.80%	4.90%		56%
Amplitude	8.70%	7.70%		89%
Slack	8.60%	3.40%		40%
MongoDB	7.80%	7.30%	5.80%	94%
Pagerduty	7.10%	7.10%	7.10%	100%
FreshWorks	7.08%	<5%		
Toast	6.96%	5.14%	<5%	74%
Box	4.10%	1.80%		44%
Avalara	3.80%	2.20%	unclear	58%
DocuSign	1.50%			
average:	15.32%	8.32%		57%

Source: https://www.saastr.com/at-the-top-saas-companies-most-co-founders-are-not-equal-and-thats-ok/

Other than the companies above, here is some more data for other global as well as Indian companies with regard to a founder's stake at IPO:

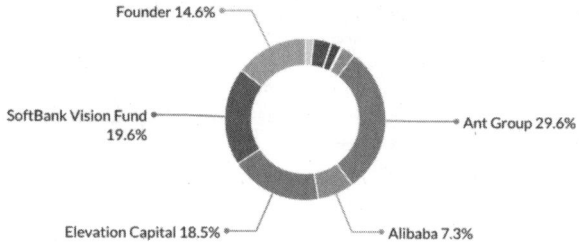

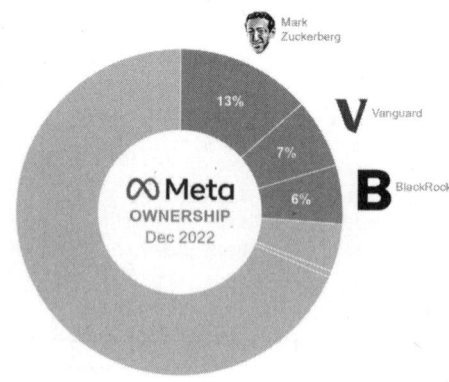

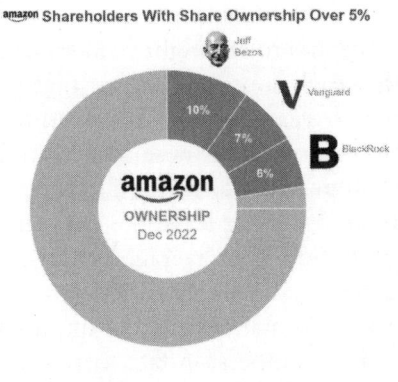

Given this data, let us therefore assume that a founder typically holds a 15 per cent stake for themselves at IPO and also an equal amount for the early team as ESOPs. That makes it a total of 30 per cent. And how many years does it typically take for a company to get to IPO? Industry data suggests that the median age to IPO is ten years.

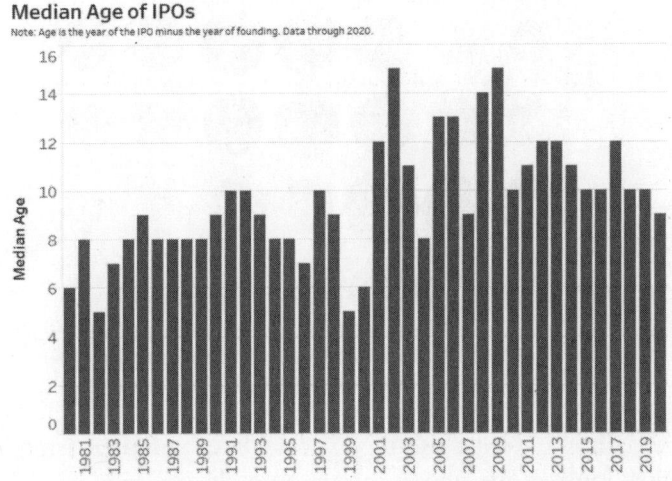

Typically, a company will bootstrap for the first two years and then raise external capital to last eight years to reach IPO. Let us also assume that each round of capital that the company raises lasts them two years. In the intervening eight years to IPO then, they will need to raise four rounds of equity funding. Now, if 30 per cent of the equity is reserved for the founder and team at IPO, that leaves 70 per cent that can be diluted over four rounds. The average equity per round by this calculation comes to 70/4 = 17.5 per cent.

While this is a mathematical calculation, it will be worth mapping whether the numbers, in fact, correspond to actual data. Here goes:

How much equity do founders give investors in each venture round?

Data from 1,229 primary priced equity rounds in 2023 | US only

Percent of all rounds in stage by dilution

Stage	Median	Under 5%	5-9.9%	10-14.9%	15-19.9%	20-24.9%	25-29.9%	30%+
Seed	20.5%	5%	9%	13%	19%	26%	15%	13%
Series A	19.5%	8%	8%	16%	20%	20%	14%	13%
Series B	17.2%	11%	14%	17%	21%	17%	9%	12%
Series C	12.6%	19%	21%	26%	13%	13%	3%	6%
Series D	10.3%	18%	32%	18%	6%	9%	12%	6%

carta data in your inbox: https://z.carta.com/data

The data is indeed close to our calculated number, isn't it? If you look at the above infographic closely, you will also notice a variation in equity dilution across different rounds. It stands to reason that you tend to dilute more in the early stages of the start-up and are able to reduce this percentage in subsequent rounds when you have more bargaining power. In fact, early-stage ventures have a 20 per cent rule of thumb, signifying the percentage dilution that typically occurs at this stage.

20% rule of thumb in early-stage venture? True.

Median equity sold to investors in primary rounds | US startups on Carta in 2023

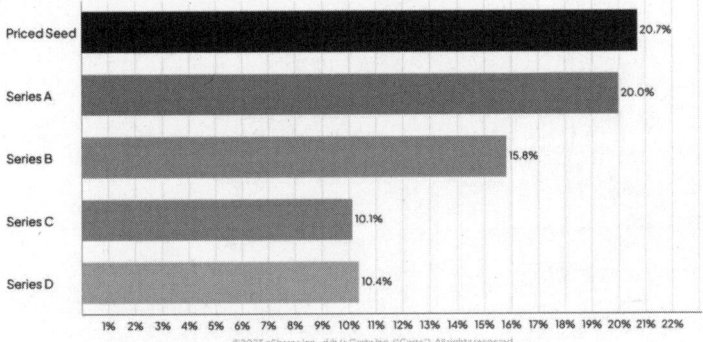

There you go, the answer to the dilution question is that, on an average, entrepreneurs tend to dilute 20 per cent in the early stage. The number tends to decrease slightly over the subsequent rounds. Eventually, at IPO, the founder typically tends to retain a 15 per cent stake for himself and an additional 15 per cent pool for the early employees.

How Are Start-Ups Valued on *Shark Tank India*?

With *Shark Tank India* bringing entrepreneurship into mainstream conversations, it will be worthwhile to end this segment with a little trivia on how valuations have panned out on the show.

Well, here is a broad synopsis of the first three seasons, which will give you a good overview of not just the success rate of pitches but also the average valuation, equity taken by angels and more.

Metric	Value
Total Pitches	157
Founders	298
Sharks	11
Pitches with Offers	58.6%
Average Valuation for Royalty Deals	INR 59 crore
Average Valuation for Non-Royalty Deals	INR 28 crore
Average Equity Offered	2.7%
Average Equity Taken	4.6%
Average Sacrifice in Valuation	~40%
Founder Gender Split	70% Male, 30% Female
Founders' Relationship	32% Friends/Colleagues, 31% Solo Founders, 16% Husband-Wife
Top States for Pitches	Maharashtra (37), NCR (22), Karnataka (21)
	Insights by Dezerv

In terms of deals that have made the cut, the metrics that have worked for successful deals include:

1. TAM: in excess of $0.5 billion or Rs 4000 crore
2. Business Growth Rates: 75–100 per cent per annum
3. Founder acumen and experience

If you are toying with the idea of participating in *Shark Tank*, it will also help you to know the statistics of which shark is most likely to invest in a pitch. Peyush Bansal tends to lead the pack in terms of percentage of deals offered, followed closely by Aman Gupta, as per data below.

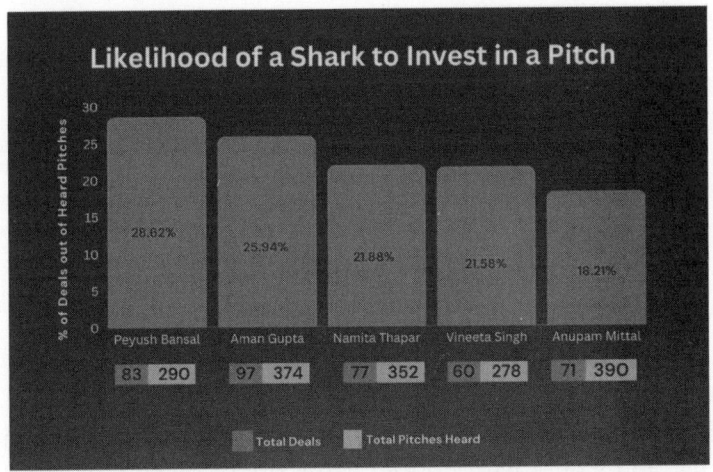

In terms of average valuation offered across the first three seasons, however, the pecking order changes with Aman Gupta leading the pack.

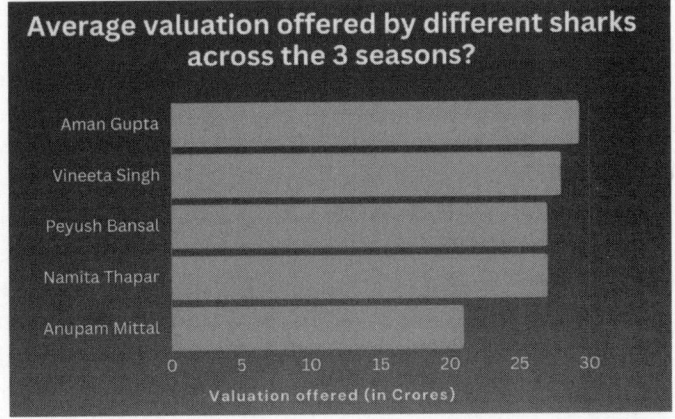

For aspiring participants on the show, here is yet another important bit of information. Turns out, that the deals that have clicked on the show have received half the valuation of their initial ask.

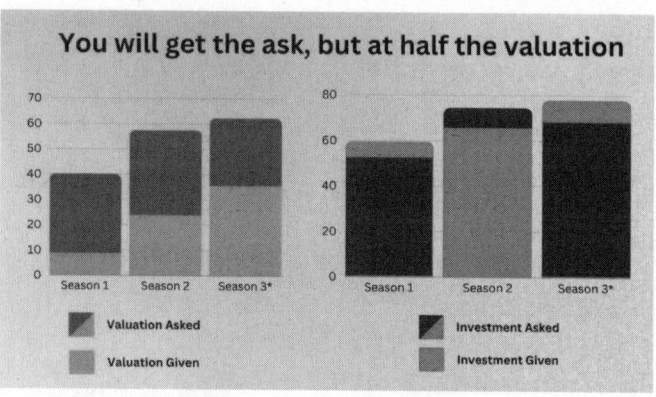

If you have been following the episodes, another trend that you would have noticed is the rise of royalty-led deals. Sharks are increasingly incorporating royalty clauses in their investment structures to protect their equity investments, especially in businesses with uncertain long-term prospects or high competition. Royalties provide investors with a recurring income stream based on the company's sales or revenue, regardless of the business's valuation or growth, offering a more secure return than relying solely on equity appreciation. As for the average valuation figures on *Shark Tank India* for non-royalty versus royalty deals, they stand at Rs 28 crore and Rs 59 crore, respectively.

With this, we come to the end of this segment on valuation. I must state here, in all fairness, that the content does not even remotely come close to covering everything about the topic. This is a highly simplified take on the subject, considering the needs of start-up founders. My hope and conviction are that reading this chapter thoroughly would equip you with the right mental framework to approach valuation. It will help you take decisions and manage negotiations in a more informed manner, and possibly save you from the pitfalls a few unfortunate entrepreneurs weren't lucky to avoid.

Section Five

Funding Brass Tacks

- Investor Outreach
- Creating a Pitch Deck
- Understanding and Negotiating Term Sheets

Having gone through the fundamentals of funding and valuation, it is now time to get to the brass tacks. How do you really reach out to investors with your proposal, what should a pitch deck focus on, and having received an interest, how do you negotiate term sheets?

Investor Outreach

Sometime in January 2022, a founder approached me to guide him on raising funds for his start-up. During a conversation, he made an interesting comment, 'Investors want to make profits, but they seem to instantly reject most of the start-ups that approach them. How do they understand what will work if they reject so quickly?'

I understood where that came from. I asked him if he knew what the acceptance rate of Y Combinator, a renowned start-up accelerator, is. He made a close guess of 2 per cent. It is now close to 1 per cent or, in a lot of cohorts, even lower. The situation is similar for all large investors. Every week, between sixty to 100 start-ups send an email to any well-known VC firm with their pitch deck. Out of them, the firm may choose to meet five or six and finally invest in one or two. For that matter, the first season of *Shark Tank India* received as many as 62,000 applications, out of which 198 businesses were selected to pitch their ideas, out of which 67 businesses received a funding commitment—that's a 0.1 per cent success rate if you went by the total number of applications.

Given the above statistics, start-up founders need to approach investors strategically, focusing on research, tailored pitches and building relationships, rather than simply 'throwing darts'. Most founders, however, when they start reaching out to investors, take a haphazard approach. They try to connect with anyone and everyone they can and miss out on the more probable opportunities due to poor planning or lack of preparedness. I understand this hustle mindset, but founders can ill-afford to waste precious time. Inefficiencies lead to longer times to completion, which, in turn, cost more money.

Let us spend some time looking at what a well-planned approach could be like.

Effective Screening

The first step is to create a list of all possible investors. If you have been following the start-up space, you'd probably be able to name a few VCs at the drop of a hat. Create a list of all investors—VCs, micro VCs, angel investors, angel syndicates, and even accelerators and incubators. For your reference, I have compiled a list of VCs, angel syndicates, accelerators and incubators as an annexure to this book.

That done, you need to effectively screen this list. Broadly, you need to look out for the following aspects:

1. **Funding activity**: Start by checking to see if the investor is actively investing in start-ups currently. If you notice that the investor hasn't invested in any start-up in the last twelve months, for instance, chances are that they are inactive presently and are unlikely to be interested.

   To figure out which VCs are actively investing in India right now, you can refer to industry reports compiled by portals such as Tracxn, Crunchbase, Pitchbook and the India Venture Capital Association (IVCA).

   Here are some sample templates as an overview to what kind of information you can expect to find:

The source of the screenshots below is Tracxn in July 2024.

Date	Company	Location	Sector	Round Details	Round Amount	Co-Investors
Mar 20, 2024	Unbox Robotics	India	Consumer [+3]	Series A (Follow-on Round)	$1.99M	RedStart.Labs [+7]
Jan 29, 2024	Vidyut	India	Energy Tech [+5]	Series A (Follow-on Round)	$10M	Zephyr Peacock [+9]
Jan 29, 2024	Vidyut	India	Energy Tech [+5]	Conventional Debt (First Round)	Undisclosed	Zephyr Peacock [+5]
Jan 17, 2024	CheQ	India	FinTech	Seed (Follow-on Round)	$4.5M	Venture Highway [+2]
Dec 04, 2023	Exponent Energy	India	Energy Tech [+5]	Series B (Follow-on Round)	$26.4M	Eight Roads Ventures [+4]
Nov 14, 2023	CoverSelf	United States	FinTech [+2]	Seed (Follow-on Round)	$8.2M	Bessmert [+1]
Sep 30, 2023	Farmbox	India	High Tech [+1]	Seed (First Round)	$2.6M	Speciale Invest
Sep 29, 2023	Kapiva	India	Life Sciences [+2]	Series B (Follow-on Round)	$12.4M	Orbimed [+0]

The Money Ball

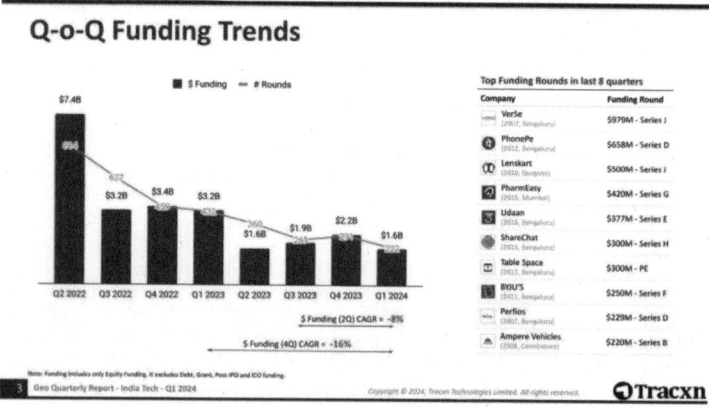

Look at when an investor last made a deal, who were the co-investors, which type of industries they invested in, at what stage of the business, and what was the total amount they raised. These points can give you a lot of insight on who is a relevant investor to pitch to, or to skip.

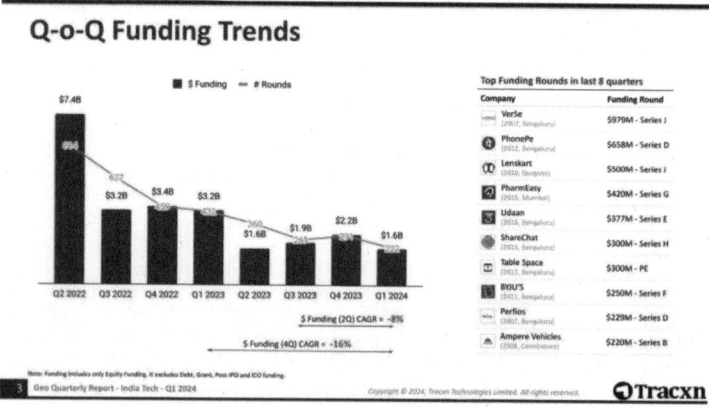

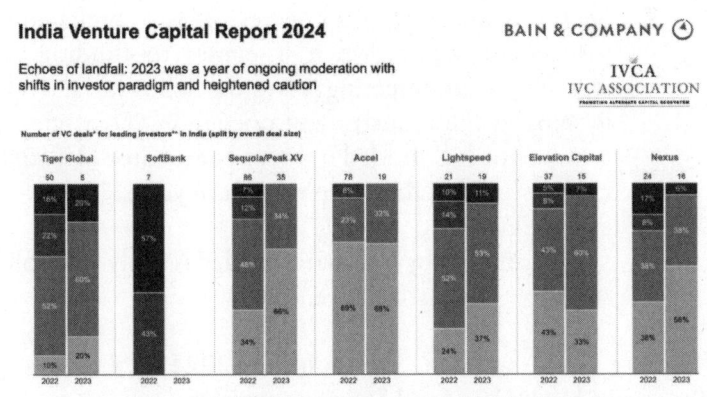

Sites like yourstory.com can also be a valuable source to keep a track of funding received by various start-ups.

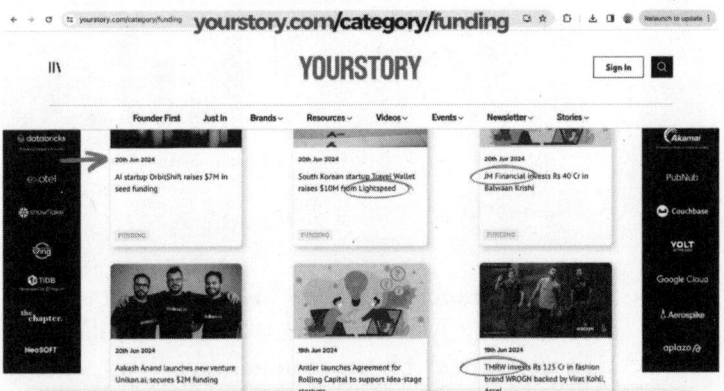

2. **Sector affiliation:** Often, investors have preferences for certain sectors when it comes to funding. It will be worth targeting investors who are actively looking at the industry you operate in. That said, if an investor has funded a direct competitor of yours, chances are that they won't invest in yours. However, exceptions exist.

    Information by industries funded is easily available. A sample template is given below.

This is a screenshot from Tracxn in July 2024 on the deals at that point by the VC fund Sauce.

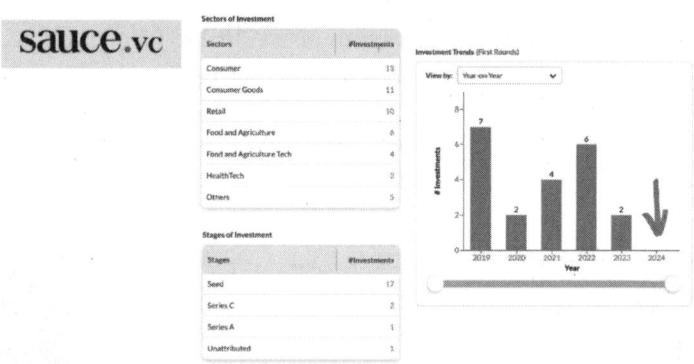

3. **Stage preference:** For every investor, check to see if they are actively funding start-ups in a similar stage as yours. Angel investors and micro VCs such as 100X.VC and Titan Capital, for example, are likely to invest in early-stage start-ups up to a maximum of Series A round, in most cases. Marquee VCs, on the other hand, usually come in at Series A and beyond, and private equity players come in even later.

    If you look at the templates shared above from sauce.vc as well as 3one4 Capital, you will also notice that the investments have been categorized by whether they are first rounds or follow-on rounds. Needless to say, that if you are looking at raising capital for the first time, you will need to focus on VCs that are actively funding first rounds.

4. **Geography preference**: This becomes relevant if you're targeting international investors. Check if their past investments indicate an interest in India (or wherever you're building), or if they have made any media statements suggesting an increased interest in your geography.

Other factors include the market conditions and the fund status of the investor. For instance, investors are more cautious in deploying funds into start-ups in bear markets. They become more rigorous with screening and valuations since the perceived risk of investing in these times is higher than usual.

VCs also have a limit to the funds they can invest. If they have already deployed most of their available funds, they may not be left with enough to invest in your company, even if everything else works in your favour. This may be hard to figure if they operate in relative stealth.

Scorecard

While we have discussed the various parameters that contribute to the probability of an investor being interested in your start-up, here is a scorecard you can create for yourself that will come in handy. All you need to do is give each investor a score of 0, 0.5, or 1 on each variable, depending on how closely they match your start-up. If there's a perfect match, it's a 1, and on no match, you give it 0.

In the table below, for instance, 'Industry match' considers how active or bullish an investor is about the industry you operate in. 'Stage match' considers how actively an investor invests in the stage of your start-up. 'Activity match' is simply about how active the investor has been in general with funding start-ups. 'Priority group' indicates how aspirational a particular investor is for you. If you are keen to associate with someone, you give them a 1, and if you're indifferent about their involvement, you probably give them a 0.

Needless to say, you can customize the scorecard template as per your requirements. The final score gives an indication of the investors you probably want in your cap table. The closer this number is to 4 (assuming you are going with four parameters), the higher it should rank in your priority.

S. No.	Investor	Industry match	Stage match	Activity match	Priority group	Final priority score
1	Sequoia	1	0	0.5	1	2.5
2	Blume	0.5	1	1	1	3.5
3	Elevation	0.5	0.5	0.5	1	2.5
4	Accel	1	0.5	1	1	3.5
5	Titan	1	1	1	1	4
6	Better	0	0	1	1	2
7	Angel 1	1	0.5	1	0.5	3
8	Angel 2	0.5	1	0.5	0.5	2.5

How to Reach Out to VCs and Ask for Their Time and Money

A list handy, you now need to get to the process of actually contacting the VCs. To do that, you will need to go ahead and look for decision-makers in each of these places.

Warm Introductions

The best-case scenario, of course, is if you know a decision-maker yourself. In such a case, you can reach out to them directly as there's already a level of credibility established. The next best alternative is to try to find a warm connection who could introduce you to the right person. It could be someone you know who's working with that firm, any founder you know who was invested in by them, or any other credible acquaintance willing to put in a good word. Colleagues, whether current or former, a common professional acquaintance or a fellow alum of your alma mater are other ways to get introduced. Keep in mind that your first impression will somehow be connected with the person making the introduction. So, if it's not someone you regard, it's probably better to explore other ways. If the person making the introduction is regarded highly by the investors, the probability of a response increases. I know about investors who have only funded start-ups that were introduced to them by someone credible. Data also suggests that warm introductions have a 16x higher chance of deal closure than cold emails.

Pro tip: This may sound counterintuitive at first glance, but it works best to connect with the low-priority investors first. These interactions will serve as practice for improvement. Since they are low priority, your stakes are lower if they don't invest. This ensures that by the time you reach out to your high-priority investors, you are habituated to the process, have received enough feedback on your pitch, and are better prepared to impress the ones that matter.

The above discussion holds good if you have a robust network; if not, then it might be prudent to build one through start-up networking events, for instance. If you can impress someone influential with your idea and performance, there's a chance they will agree to introduce you to the right people.

Although this doesn't fall under the ambit of 'warm introductions', another way to attract interest is through social media activity. Post about what you do and your progress, and share insights. You are more likely to be spotted by an investor or an analyst working at any of the VC firms if you're consistent. However, ensure that your personal branding is consistent with your start-up's. If you post derogatory or cringeworthy content, for instance, you'll get eyeballs at the expense of your brand. It will do more harm than good.

Other mediums to similarly grab attention are AngelList—list your start-up here and post updates, job openings, etc. You could also consider listing your start-up on a portal such as Tracxn or aim to get published in credible media platforms like YourStory, Inc42, *Economic Times, Mint* and the like.

Cold Outreach

Getting a response from cold outreaches is, admittedly, challenging especially since marquee investors are flooded with hundreds of emails. It's humanly impossible for an already busy individual to read or even skim through all of them. That said, you can work through the probability and do what's in your control to maximize your chances.

One way to improve your chances is to skim through LinkedIn. With a diligent search, you may come across people who could have shared their contact details and even indicated that they are open to receiving cold emails.

Sample this:

Having found the contact details, the initial email that you send out is crucial. Allie Janoch, founder of a SaaS start-up called Mapistry, shared in a Medium post about her first failed attempt to get the attention of investor Jason Lemkin from SaaStr. The email she shot is shared here.

Allie Janoch <allie@mapistry.com> 10/1/15
to jason

Hi Jason,
Thanks for chatting with me for a few minutes yesterday at Berkeley about "uber for enterprise". The "uber for enterprise" thesis really hit home for me, it's exactly what we're doing at Mapistry by replacing environmental consultants and professionals.

> We are doing $2K in MRR at the moment, but I would love to talk to you more when we get 10x revenue. I know you don't typically grab coffee with companies until you are ready to invest, so can I reach out to you in a few months when we are ready to discuss investment?
>
> Thanks,
> Allie Janoch CEO | Mapistry

About this outreach, she writes:

I made the email somewhat personal and mentioned something that he had talked about during the event. But a lot is missing. Didn't explain what Mapistry does, I alluded to it, but didn't provide a clear explanation. In the second paragraph, I was pretty self-deprecating, which looking back at, I hate. I didn't brag about our progress; I mentioned our MRR but essentially said 'our traction is pretty lame, and I'm sure you wouldn't want to talk to me now,' might be true, but why did I say it? Finally, my ask is awful. 'Can I reach out to you in a few months . . .'

That isn't an actionable ask. Plus, I didn't follow up in a few months! Overall, the email comes off as unconfident and vague.

Two years later, however, she claims she was more ready and confident and adopted an approach that eventually worked. She shot an email to the same investor and got a response within a few hours.

Date: Thu, Oct 19, 2017 at 5:50 PM
Subject: Mapistry – SaaS for environmental regulations – Fortune 500 Customers – Seed

Hi Jason,
My name is Allie, and I am the CEO of Mapistry. Mapistry is a SaaS application for environmental regulations at industrial facilities. Environmental regulations are notoriously confusing and complicated, yet the technology used to manage them is usually no more sophisticated than excel spreadsheets and email. This system leaves manufacturing companies vulnerable to multi-million dollar lawsuits and severe damage to their brand.

Traction & numbers:

- **customers include Fortune 500 companies like 3M, Republic Services, Tesla and Procter & Gamble**
- growing 15% month over month
- September revenue: $67K
- fully ramped, our existing customer base corresponds to a $4M run rate.
- United States TAM: $3.7B ($1T environmental market globally)

You can check out more details about Mapistry in a short deck here.

I am raising a seed round of funding for Mapistry to maximize on our recent momentum, expand our product to other environmental domains (focused on stormwater to date), and continue to develop software that automates services traditionally provided by environmental consultants.

I've been following SaaStr for a while. In particular, I saw your talk with Veeva from the SaaStr conference and I'd love to talk to

> you about how we fit into this trend of vertical SaaS. One of the reasons so few companies are using software for environmental compliance is that the only tools available are so unspecific and horizontal that the customizations required are so immense, they become unrealistic.
>
> I liked what Peter had to say about services. We also feel very strongly that we have great people and we aren't going to give their time away for free. We like to think of our environmental services as being paid for sales and/or customer success. In fact, I just did a quick, back of the envelope calculation, and looks like we've been doing about 35% profit margins on our services for 2017, which has been a nice source of revenue for the rest of the company while we get off the ground.
>
> I'd love to schedule a time for a 30-minute phone call or coffee. Do you have any time the week after next?
>
> Allie Janoch
> CEO | Mapistry

Source: Allie Janoch's article on Medium

She writes:

For each investor I emailed, whether it was an intro or cold, I modified the template to personalize it for them. For Jason, who was my number one choice for an investor, I spent a couple of hours researching and putting together the later part of the email.

Apparently, the recipient, Jason Lemkin, said this about the email:

'It does a good job of summarizing the opportunity, early customers and traction, growth profile, and market size. Perhaps just as importantly, it is truly personalized.

'Also for me at least, it's low drama. "Do you have any time the week after next?" The confident and relatively data-rich but low drama emails work best. Knowing there's little time it's much less risky to meet a founder you've barely met before and dig in.'

However, you must take into account that every individual has their own preference, and one's views won't apply to all. It usually takes time to perfect your cold-emailing template to receive maximum responses. Since it's bound to take a few hits and misses, that's another reason to practise these with low-priority investors. When they start getting you meetings, you can then move up the order with a refined approach.

Karan Bajaj, founder of WhiteHat Jr, stated in his blog that he approached investors only through cold outreaches on LinkedIn. He shared an example of the template that he claimed got six out of ten VCs to respond.

Anup Gupta
Looking forward to partnering with entrepreneurs pursuing breakthr...

Anup Gupta   1st
Looking forward to partnering with entrepreneurs pursuing breakthrough opportunities across sectors, Nexus Venture Partners

Karan Bajaj   8:08 AM
Anup—I'm Discovery India CEO. 15 years excellent operating experience, wrote 3 novels with Penguin/Harper, all bestsellers +movie deals. I see things through. Would love to meet with you for advice on a ed-tech venture if amenable
Karan

> **Anup Gupta   8:08 AM**
> Hello Karan - nice to emeet, pls send me some details
>
> Rgds, Anup

He further writes: 'Contrary to public perception, I found almost all Indian venture capitalists extremely responsive and courteous, both in their acceptance and rejection.'[*]

This is obviously an encouraging statement for founders. But know that this comes from someone who wrote good cold messages and was already a highly distinguished professional when he started out. His credentials allowed him to reach out to decision-makers directly and request for a meeting. For someone less experienced, it may not be the greatest idea, especially if you haven't tested the waters and received interest from other low-priority investors.

Allie Janoch elaborated the elements of a cold email template in her blog, which I have slightly modified and summarized in the pointers below.

- A crisp subject line that quickly but effectively explains the purpose of the email; also helps if you name the investor here
- Explain the problem you're solving as easily and simply as possible
- Mention the most important traction numbers and other impressive facts (e.g. stellar team, product demo link) as bullet points
- A clear reason for raising money and what you intend to achieve with it

---

[*] Source: Karan Bajaj's blog post 'How to Raise Start-up Funding with No Product'.

- End with a clear request for a 30-minute call or a meeting and give enough time so that the recipient doesn't feel rushed
- Attach your deck with the email

Some additional pointers:

- Make the email personal—it should never feel like a copy-pasted template
- Be brief—minimize the usage of words and make information more palatable by using bullet points and numbers
- Send emails to five or six investors on the same day to increase the probability of securing at least one meeting in the next few days.

Here is a template I have used myself. As you would notice, the business highlights and performance metrics are presented upfront by way of crisp bullet points as no one has the patience to go over large paragraphs.

Sarthak Ahuja <casarthakahuja@gmail.com>   Tue, Jan 30, 1:54PM
to Apoorv, Aditi, Chirag

Hi Apoorv,
This is in reference to our message exchange last evening.

I handle Investor Relations at Burma Burma and wanted to understand if Guild Capital would be interested in an investment opportunity for the company's second and final round of equity funding.

A few highlights about the business are as under:
- India's only, and the world's largest Burmese cuisine chain
- 11 restaurants across 8 cities in India, and 1 upcoming in a week

> - Forbes 30U30 Founder, and 4.8 star ratings across Zomato
> - Raised a USD 3 Mn as growth capital in 9th year of operations
>
> **Current Performance - December 2023**
> - Rs 100 cr ARR achieved - 2X in one year
> - 22% operating profit at restaurant level - highest in the category
> - Food cost optimized below 20% of Net Revenue
> - Doubled Footprint from 6 to 12 restaurants in one financial year
> - EBITDA profitable company generating positive cash flows
>
> The company has recently been published in Forbes, and you can read the story here.
>
> I have attached the company deck for your reference and perusal. Let me know any available time slots for the coming week so that we can schedule a call.
>
> Thanks,
> **Sarthak Ahuja**

Having sent the emails, do realize that investors will probably not respond to your first cold outreach. In such cases, wait for about three to four days before politely sending a follow-up. If you have any new information to add, use this email as the opportunity to share it. You can consider sharing a line about your start-up again as a quick reminder of what you're building. It makes it easier for the investor to grasp the idea than plainly asking them to 'refer to the trailing mail'. The chances of responses to follow-up emails are higher, especially when asked politely and professionally. It also somewhat indicates the tenacity of the founder. But again, ensure there's a clear line between tenacity and desperation. Don't follow up in intervals shorter than three days, and don't be too repetitive if there's no response.

Data indicates that you will need this tenacity not only at the VC contact stage but throughout your fundraising journey.

If a VC received 100 pitches through email a week, they choose to get their analysts on calls with only about a quarter of these. Just about ten pitches may get a second meeting with someone senior from the fund. And while VCs may do due diligence on five out of the 100, only one may eventually get a term sheet.

Deals Received	100
Analyst Meeting	28
Partner Meeting	10
Due Diligence	5
Term Sheet	1

Creating a Pitch Deck

Other than the introductory email, the pitch deck is really the first document that represents your start-up. It can therefore make or break your fundraising journey. It is extremely important for you to get it right. In fact, every slide of the deck is an opportunity to build a strong case for your start-up.

The important aspect to figure out in building your pitch deck is what does an investor want to see in it. Most marquee VCs have published and recommended formats for early-stage pitch decks. All of them broadly seek the same information albeit in different order. Sequoia, now Peak XV, for instance, recommends the following flow:

- Company Purpose
- Problem
- Solution
- Why Now
- Market Size

- Competition
- Product
- Founding Team
- Business Model
- Financials

An old recommended format by Accel Partners available on SlideShare goes like this:

- Team
- Product
- Customers
- More Product Details
- Market Size
- Competition
- Current Status
- Execution Plan

Remember there is no magic template that can impress everyone. You will need to create pitch decks for every funding round and customize them for different investors. The first version of the pitch deck, however, will benefit from these elements:

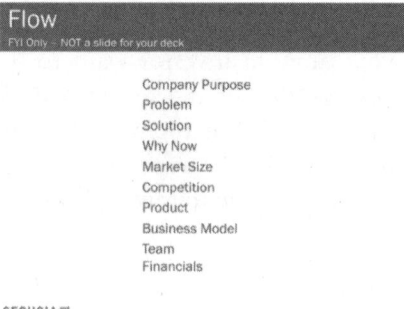

Let us get into the details of how you can effectively present each of these elements.

Company Purpose

Ideally you should be able to effectively describe the company/business purpose in a single declarative sentence. Some examples should make this clear.

Here is how White Hat Jr, an online platform that provides live, one-on-one coding, math and music classes for kids, describes its purpose or mission:

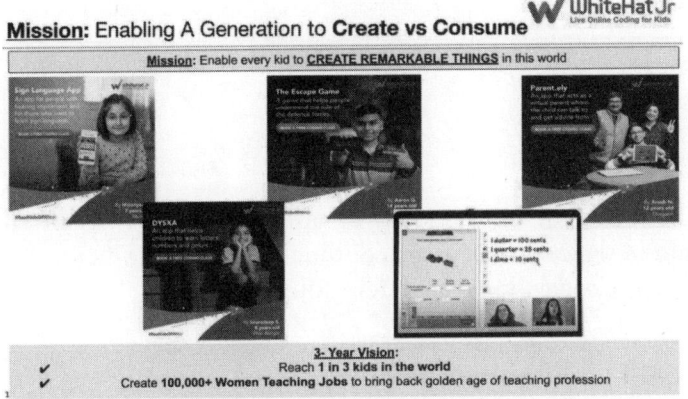

Here is a similar example from Remi, a platform that helps remote teams build culture and connection easily and effectively.

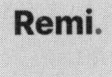

The world has changed, and remote work is here to stay

68m people will be working remotely 3+ days a week by 2025 in Europe & US alone

25% of enterprises expecting more than half of their organizations' **workforce to predominantly work from home post Covid-19**

Source: Statista/Gartner 2020

Problem

The 'Problem' slide should be able to able to describe the pain of the customer as also outline how the customer tackles the issue today. Here are a few potent examples:

Remi's problem statement:

The problem

80%* of the people we spoke to said:

"When working remotely, it's difficult to build and maintain social connection with my team."

*based on 100+ interviews with remote workers in October-December 2020

Here's how Beelinguapp, a language learning app, presents the problem faced by learners:

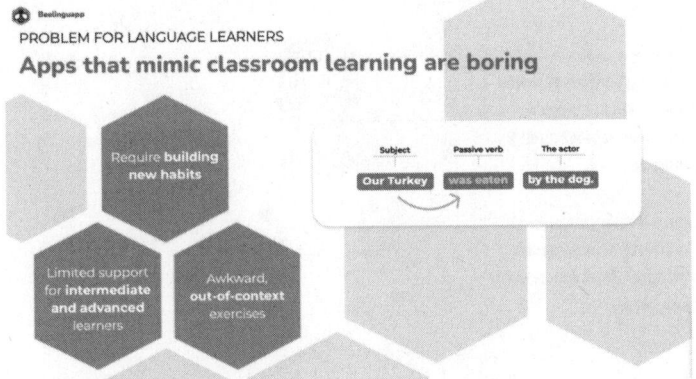

The key lies in not using complex and wordy problem statements. The objective of this slide is that the investor should be able to infer that you have picked up a genuine problem. At a later date when you go on to present the pitch in front of the investors, if relevant, you can narrate the story of how you faced the issue yourself and took it upon yourself to solve it. It will be evidence of your internal drive and motivation, and the investor's conviction in you is likely to go up several notches.

Solution and Why Now

It is time now to demonstrate your company's value proposition to make the customer's life better. It will help to show where your product physically sits and to offer use cases. The 'Why Now' slide needs to follow this up with the historical evolution of the category. You need to define recent trends that make your solution feasible.

Here is Remi's solution:

Here is yet another solution slide, by way of an example, of a no-code tool that aids content creators:

Market Size

The objective of every investor is to find the next big opportunity to make money. The strongest indicator of such market opportunities is the market size. The slide, therefore, should present the TAM (top down), SAM (bottoms up) and SOM.

Here's how Airbnb presented the market size in its pitch deck:

Source: Piktochart

This is how we presented market size for a client in edtech:

Notice how in the above slide we have used different methods to arrive at the market size for India. One, where we have calculated the number of schoolgoing kids in urban households where the income is more than Rs 10 lakh. In the other, we have first estimated the number of school-going kids in urban areas and then divided them as per the amount they spent on schooling annually. In both approaches, the number of kids totalled 22 million. The average spending on schooling multiplied by this number gave them the market size for India.

Competition

There are several methods of presenting competition. An effective one is the 2x2 matrix. The two axes represent two competitive advantages while you place your start-up and its competitors in different quadrants. Somewhat like this:

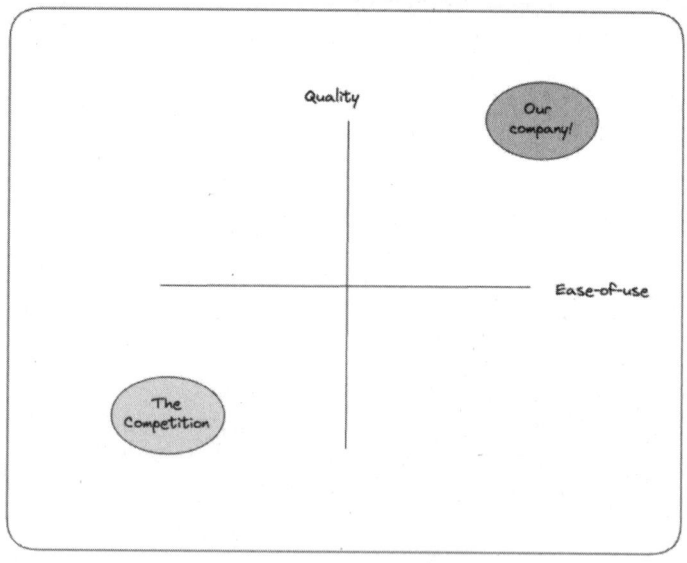

Here's how Airbnb used the four-quadrant system to create their competition slide:

Source: Piktochart

Here is yet another effective way to list your features/benefits vis-à-vis competition:

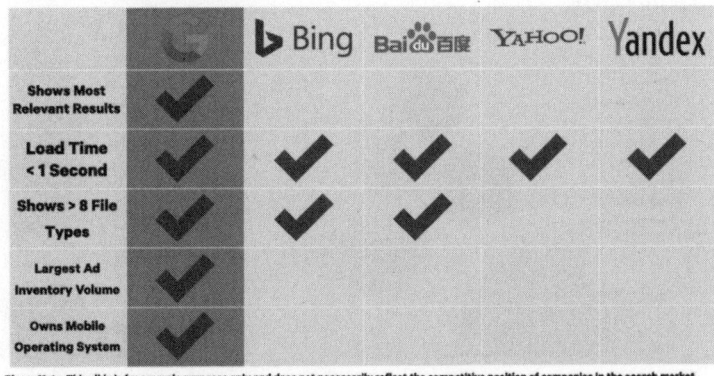

Product

The product slide needs to delineate the product line-up in terms of form factor, functionality, features, architecture, intellectual property and more.

Sample some of these slides that represent different types of products across a range of industries:

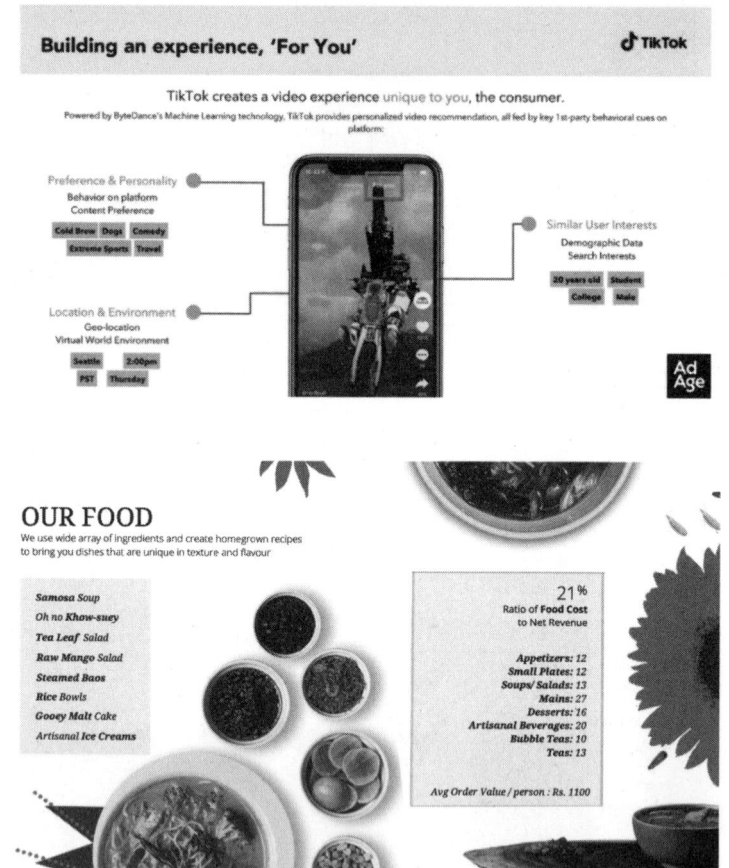

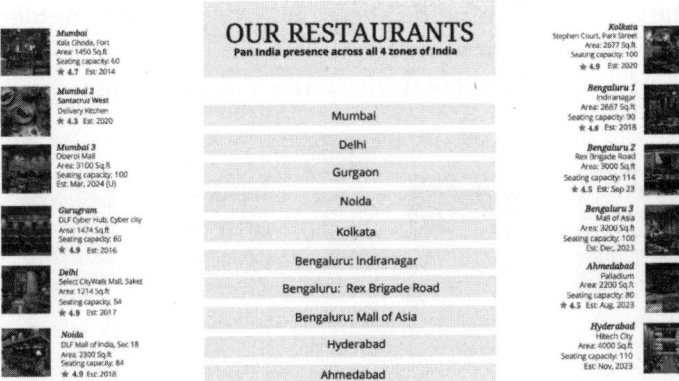

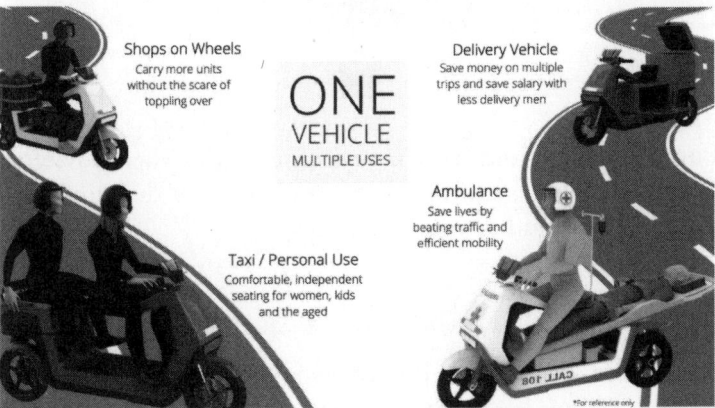

Founding Team

When an investor looks at the team slide of the pitch deck, they are looking to assess the following aspects:

- Execution capabilities
- Commitment
- Team capability

The objective of this slide, therefore, is to establish credibility in the eyes of the investor.

Here is an example that effectively achieves this:

Founders sometimes also mention names of their advisers; if they are highly accomplished people in your domain, they will definitely add to your credibility.

Business Model

This slide could include the following information:

- Revenue Model
- Pricing
- Average Account Size/Lifetime Value
- Sales and Distribution Model
- Customer List/Pipeline

Sample the slides below to get an idea of how you can effectively convey the broad business model without the slides being too verbose. Once again, the examples have been chosen from across industry verticals for you to appreciate how a variety of business models can find effective representation.

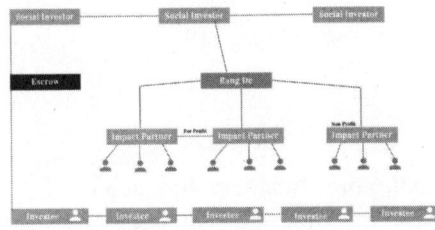

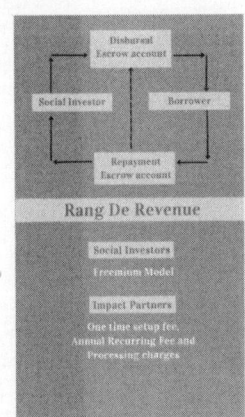

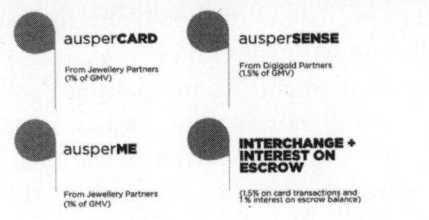

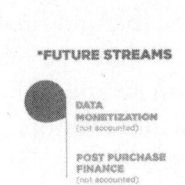

Business Model
Build a brand in 7 days

End-to-end tools to ◎ **Launch** ◎ **Build** ◎ **Scale** Creator led D2C Brands

Phase 1: Responsibilities: Take 20+ Creators to $20 Mn ARR		Phase 2: Fund and take a bigger stake in our winners and help them scale	
House of X	**Creator**	**House of X**	**Creator**
Full stack platform	Logo, Design, Brand Story	Operations	Marketing
Ideation & brand building playbook	Place small initial order	Finance and Accounting	Performance marketing
Sourcing needs	Marketing	Capital	Distribution
Packaging & Fulfilment	(Through their own social network)	Creative Strategy	Storytelling
Payment Gateway	Distribution	Customer Delight	
Shipping + E-commerce		Business Planning	
Customer Support			

Financials

These slides describe what your business has achieved to date in terms of business metrics. The metrics that are typically needed to indicate the financial health of your company include:

- P&L
- Balance Sheet
- Cash Flow Statement

Besides the financials, this segment should also indicate your cap table and finally end with your ask.

While you may think of cutting and pasting Excel sheets to these slides, it is better not to. The idea is, once again, for the investors to get a quick overview of the financials as opposed to going through reams of numbers at this stage. The proof as they say lies in the pudding. Here is an example: this time from the restaurant business. You will notice how the slides give a broad overview of the health of the business at one glance.

Funding Brass Tacks

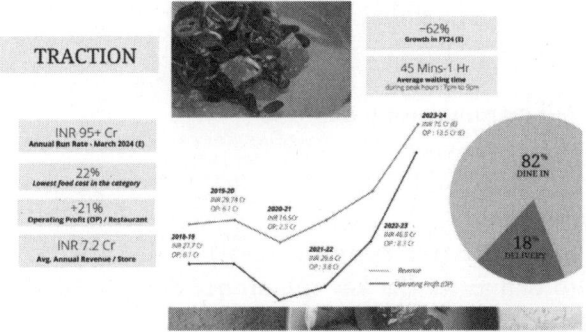

TRACTION

INR 95+ Cr
Annual Run Rate - March 2024 (E)

22%
Lowest food cost in the category

+21%
Operating Profit (OP) / Restaurant

INR 7.2 Cr
Avg. Annual Revenue / Store

-62%
Growth in FY24 (E)

45 Mins-1 Hr
Average waiting time
during peak hours : 7pm to 9pm

2019-20 INR 29.78 Cr / OP: 6.1 Cr
2020-21 INR 14.50 / OP: 2.5 Cr
2018-19 INR 27.7 Cr / OP: 6.1 Cr
2021-22 INR 26.6 Cr / OP: 3.8 Cr
2022-23 INR 46.5 Cr / OP: 8.3 Cr
2023-24 INR 75 Cr (E) / OP: 13.5 Cr (E)

— Revenue
— Operating Profit (OP)

82% DINE IN
18% DELIVERY

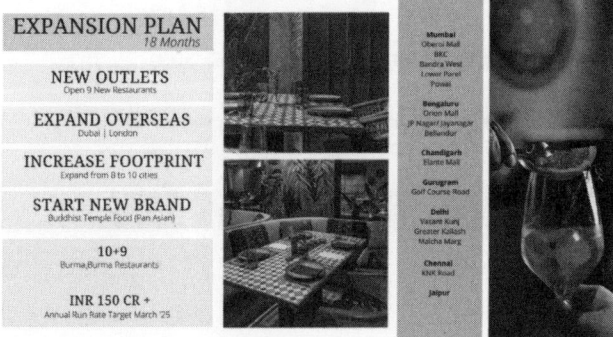

EXPANSION PLAN
18 Months

NEW OUTLETS
Open 9 New Restaurants

EXPAND OVERSEAS
Dubai | London

INCREASE FOOTPRINT
Expand from 8 to 10 cities

START NEW BRAND
Burkdhist Temple Food (Pan Asian)

10+9
Burma Burma Restaurants

INR 150 CR +
Annual Run Rate Target March '25

Mumbai
Oberoi Mall
BKC
Bandra West
Lower Parel
Powai

Bengaluru
Orion Mall
JP Nagar | Jayanagar
Bellundur

Chandigarh
Elante Mall

Gurugram
Golf Course Road

Delhi
Vasant Kunj
Greater Kailash
Malcha Marg

Chennai
KNK Road

Jaipur

GOING FORWARD

4 Year Plan Burma Burma + New Brand	Y1	Y2	Y3	Y4
Annual Run Rate (Rs. Crores)	86	150	215	288
No. of Outlets	11	20	28	36
Revenue / Restaurant (Rs. Cr)	7.2	7.5	7.7	8

As for the Ask slide, you broadly need to state three main points:

1. The fundraising amount
2. The runway
3. The use of funds

Here is an effective template that not only states the ask but also delineates the key milestones that the funding will help achieve.

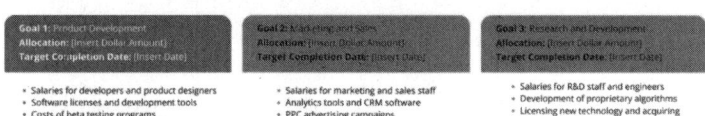

If you already have other investors on board who have agreed to invest in the ongoing round, you must also mention the committed amounts by these investors and the balance left to be raised. Similarly, you can also mention your past investors in a separate slide.

Presenting the Pitch

While what we have discussed so far are the elements of a pitch deck, you also need to make sure that you are ready to present the pitch once you are led to the next step, namely an investor meeting. It is important to remember that you are dealing with people who are very smart and also hard-pressed for time. To stand out, you must make them feel that their time spent listening to you is worth it.

For one, you surely need to be a good storyteller. Business storytelling is all about presenting facts in context and delivering them with a certain amount of emotion. If you go back and think of any presentations that have stayed in your memory, it surely isn't because of the bullet points it laid out but because of the compelling story the narrator presented. There is brain chemistry at play here. Storytelling is known to trigger the release of hormones like dopamine, oxytocin and cortisol, which contribute to emotional engagement, memory formation and empathy.

In terms of pitches, per se, try and recall the pitches from *Shark Tank*, for instance. The ones that come to your mind will surely be the ones that had a compelling story. You would remember the pitch of Jugaadu Kamlesh, for instance. He wasn't the most suave of all candidates but had an emotional plea, humour, authenticity and more that endeared him and his story to you.

Andy Raskin, who helps build strategic narratives for CEOs and business leaders, suggests a wonderful storytelling framework in a Medium article.[*] Here are some of the elements he recommends:

- **Name the Enemy**: Do not start the pitch talking about yourself or your product. Instead, begin the pitch with the biggest impediment to the customer's happiness in

---

[*] Andy Raskin, 'Want a Better Pitch? Watch this.', Medium, 13 July 2015, https://medium.com/firm-narrative/want-a-better-pitch-watch-this-328b95c2fd0b

the current scenario. As far as possible, paint an emotional picture of how the lives of people can change.
- **Answer 'Why Now':** Explain why the timing is perfect to change the status quo.
- **Show the promised land before explaining how you will get there:** Essentially explain what the better world would be like for the target audience. Don't just mention the functional benefits yet, show the outcomes of those benefits.
- **Identify obstacles and how you propose to overcome them:** Don't worry about delineating the genuine obstacles. In fact, they are likely to hold audience's interest.
- **Present evidence to show your capability:** Demonstrate what you have built and the results you have attained. If there is a live product, bring it along. If it is a tech product, be sure to present a demo.

Meeting Hacks

Etiquette expert Sara Jane Ho tells her clients that when evaluating a potential partner or a date for a romantic relationship, it mostly takes people no more than two seconds of the first impression to make their decision.

And once a poor impression is formed, it takes eight meetings to reverse it! Eight meetings! Now, with an investor, you may not have that luxury. You get a thirty-minute slot with an investor after a warm connect or a series of cold emails, and within the first five to seven minutes of observing the conversation, I can mostly tell whether the founder will get a yes or no.

I strongly recommend that you be prepared to answer the following questions in less than sixty seconds each if any of them are thrown at you during an investor pitch:

1. What's your target customer persona?
2. What's your moat? How are you 10x better than your competition?
3. What's your traction?
4. When can you hit your next milestone that will double your value, and what is it?
5. What is the experience of the co-founders working together? How do you know each other?
6. What is the incremental benefit your customer is getting by using your product?
7. What makes you the best-suited founder to build this?
8. If this is the only round of funding you get, can you survive without any more funding? How fast will you turn profitable and break even?
9. What is your gross margin, contribution margin and unit level economics?
10. What's that one revenue vertical in your business model that contributes the most to profitability?
11. What's your customer acquisition cost, and what have you done to lower it?
12. What exit plan do you have for the investor?
13. What are the complementary skills of the co-founders/founding team?

How Many Pitches and Meetings Does It Take?

While we have been discussing the elements of a pitch deck and how you could present it, the one question that is likely to be running in your mind all the time is how many pitches and/or meetings does it take to actually close a round.

It stands to reason that the number of meetings and pitches it takes varies with the investor as well as your idea and product. Statistically, you will have to pitch to at least thirty to forty investors to get an expression of interest. The process tends to become smoother after that as the first one helps you attract more willing investors to take the bet.

In 2015, Brian Chesky, the co-founder and CEO of Airbnb, published an article on Medium titled '7 Rejections':

On June 26, 2008, our friend Michael Seibel introduced us to 7 prominent investors in Silicon Valley. We were attempting to raise $150,000 at a $1.5M valuation. That means for $150,000 you could have bought 10 per cent of Airbnb. Below you will see 5 rejections. The other 2 did not reply.

---

to Brian, Joe, Nathan   7/16/08

Thank you for the introduction. Brian good to meet you -- while this sounds interesting it is not something we would do here -- not in our area of focus, do wish you best of luck

---

to Brian, Joe, Nathan   8/1/08

Hi Brian,
Apologies for the delayed response. We've had a chance to discuss internally, and unfortunately don't think that it's the right opportunity for from an investment perspective. The potential market opportunity did not seem large enough for our required model.

---

to Brian   7/30/08

Brian:
I ran this by my partner. First, it's not in one of our prime 5 target markets so it's a long shot for our involvement. Also, since it's not an area where we are currently investing, getting us involved doesn't give you the expertise that would be best for your company.

> My recommendation is to keep us posted. If you get to the point of a Series A investment please let us know and we'll take a look.

---

to Brian, Joe, Nathan						9/2/08

Brian
Thanks for the follow up. I was unavailable to get on the call today as I'll be out of town through end of day Thursday. I really like the progress you guys have made, but between issues outstanding with ABB and my current time commitments to other projects, specifically existing investments, I'm not going to be able to proceed with an investment at this point. My biggest remaining concerns are:

- significant ramp up in traction post the DNC and RNC
- technical staffing
- investment syndicate

---

to Brian							10/28/08

Brian
We decided yesterday to not take this to the next level
We've always struggled with travel as a category
We recognize its one of the top e-commerce categories but for some reason, we've not been able to get excited about travel related businesses

'The investors that rejected us were smart people, and I am sure we didn't look very impressive at the time. Next time you have an idea and it gets rejected, I want you to think of these emails.'

Notice that two of these emails are over three months apart, so you know it may take months of convincing and the outcome may still not be in your favour. You can look at these emails and get either inspired or dejected, but as a founder looking to raise funds, you must have a thick skin to absorb such rejections and continue improving.

While on the subject of rejections, it is also important to understand the different ways of refusal. Some investors offer a direct 'No', which is clear and allows you to move on immediately. Others give some variation of 'not now'. And then there are a few who give no response or ghost you. If a few follow-ups don't elicit any response, consider it a refusal to invest and move on. However, you can continue keeping them in the loop with your progress updates, especially the more desirable ones. Designing small and effective feedback loops helps you become efficient in the process and allows you to refine the approach faster.

Overall, what you can do to make the process efficient is track your efforts and outcomes with different investors. An example of such a tracker is given here.

Investor	Priority Score	Contact identified	Email 1	Email 2	Meeting 1	MIS Shared	Valuation	Term sheet
Investor 1	1.5							
Investor 2	1.5							
Investor 3	2							
Investor 4	2							

Each cell can also contain remarks on learnings or feedback you obtained at different points of communication. This will help you improve your approach with every new investor you get in touch with.

Pro tip: If you are repeatedly getting rejected, it is worthwhile to spend some time introspecting. It is possible that either the idea lacks merit or is not investable as a VC business. Getting feedback at the end of every such discussion by simply asking, 'Do you think this is an investable business idea?' can help you obtain clarity early. If they think it's not, then you can follow up with, 'What do you think can make this idea investable?' If you get similar suggestions from all the investors you speak with, see if any of those can be implemented in your business to make it more investable. However, do it only if it makes proper business sense to you and is aligned with why you started out.

Before we end this segment, it will be fitting to look at a template that will help you understand how investors tend to evaluate start-ups. Go ahead and self-evaluate yourself on the parameters that the investor is sure to evaluate you on.

Company:			Date:			
Industry:		Stage:		Capital Raise:		
Brief Description:						
INVESTMENT CRITERIA			BETTER SCORE >>>>>>>>>>>>>>>>			
Criteria	**Description**		Low Score	Average/Unknown		High Score
Target Market	Clearly defined target market? Is large now or in the future? Stable or high growth? High priced niche?		1	2	3	4	5
Problem or Need	Problem / need is real? Fad / Short term trend? Sustainable pain, challenge, need?		1	2	3	4	5
Solution	Better, Faster, Cheaper? Brand? Quality? Efficient? Convenient? Unique? Price? Value Prop?		1	2	3	4	5

Team, Board, Advisors	Industry knowledge, unique skills, leadership, key relationships, prior successes and/or failures	1	2	3	4	5
Traction	Min Viable Product? LTV / CAC? Customer ROI? Key metrics? $ Raised / Revenue? Partners?	1	2	3	4	5
Competition vs. Competitive Advantages	Direct vs. indirect? Barriers to entry? Differentiation? Simpler alternative exists? Future obsolescence? Unfair or sustainable advantage? Patents? Partners? Key Risks?	1	2	3	4	5

Revenue Model	Customers or units x $ Price, Recurring or one-time? ARPU? LTV? Ways to increase? Sales cycle? High Price vs. Volume?	1	2	3	4	5
Strategy: Key Expenses / Time Efforts	Cost of Product? Improve Gross Margin? Cost & Time to Maintain Customer / Operations? CAC? Marketing Strat? Improvements?	1	2	3	4	5
Financials	Rev ARR? Gross vs. Net Rev? Gross Margins & % of revenues? LTV/CAC? Burn/mo & Runway? Path to profitability? Market penetration required?	1	2	3	4	5

Exit Opportunity	Potential Buyers? Why Buy vs. Build? IPO? Exit Multiples? Big Enough Exit Possible?	1	2	3	4	5
Investment Terms	Amount?, Pre/Post-$?, Post-$ / Revenues?, Investors?, $ committed?, Previous $ Raised & Terms?, Debt?	1	2	3	4	5
Strategic Value	How We Can Help? Directly or Indirectly Strategic? Intro's to Customers, Partners, Strategics, Investors, Employees?	1	2	3	4	5

* * *

Understanding and Negotiating a Term Sheet

The term sheet is seen as the Holy Grail for founders seeking investment. Securing one is perceived as the end of the fundraising journey for a particular round. However, this is only partially true. In this segment, we'll understand what a term sheet is and what it is not, besides looking at some of its clauses.

What Is a Term Sheet, and What It Is Not

A term sheet is a legal document that investors share with the founders after they have agreed to invest in their start-up. It is usually five to six pages long and outlines the details of the association between the investor and the start-up. It is the first point of understanding between the two parties and a skeleton for the terms and conditions based on which the investment in the start-up will take place. The term sheet is negotiated upon and finally, when the investor and the start-up both agree on the details of the investment, it gets signed.

An important aspect to remember is that a term sheet is a handshake agreement stating the terms at which an investor is putting money into a start-up. But it is not legally binding on either the investor or the start-up. Any of them can back out from the transaction until the Definitive Agreements (Shareholder's Agreement, Share Subscription Agreement, Share Purchase Agreement) are signed.

However, some of the clauses of a term sheet can be binding and you should be cautious about them. These clauses are usually related to confidentiality and no-shop. It basically safeguards the details of conversations between the two parties from being put out in the public or shared with a competitor to benefit the start-up at the investor's expense.

An investor has the right to cancel an offered term sheet when serious discrepancies emerge in the performance of the start-up during due diligence. A founder, too, can back out of a term sheet if they get a better offer of investment from a different investor.

Control Terms versus Economic Terms

Let us begin by looking at some important terms that comprise a term sheet. Broadly these terms can be categorized into control terms vs economic terms

As the names suggest, economic terms denote the clauses that impact the value of the business or the investors or the founders. They affect the valuation and dilution of the shareholding and returns of the business. Control terms, on the other hand, refer to the clauses that pertain to decision-making powers in the company.

Here is a handy classification:

Economic Terms	Control Terms
Valuation	Board of Directors
ESOP	Drag-Along Rights
Liquidation Preference	Info Rights
Promoter's Lock-In and Vesting	Reserved Matters
Antidilution Protection	Restriction of Transfer
	Right of First Offer (ROFO)
	Right of First Refusal (ROFR)

Term Sheet Clauses and Negotiation Tips

This section lays out some of the clauses of a term sheet (as available on the Start-up India website and prepared by LetsVenture) that merit some clarification. Besides explaining some of these clauses, I have also stated some pointers that could come in handy during negotiations. Here goes:

1.0 Transaction Details

1.1 **Business** The Company is engaged in the business of _____.

The term 'Business' simply states the description of the business.

Ensure that this description is the same as that given in the Memorandum of Association (MoA) of the company. Start-ups often pivot in their initial stages. It may happen that the product that you are raising funds for is not what the MoA mentions. Before you raise funds, ensure the details are aligned.

| 1.2 | **Promoter(s)** | The Company is currently controlled by [•] and [•]. |

'Promoter(s)' simply refers to the founders of the company. This clause details the cap table of the start-up.

| 1.3 | **Current Capital Structure** | The current paid up and issued share capital of the Company comprises of [•] equity shares with a face value of INR [•] per share and [•] preference shares with a face value of INR [•] per share. The Promoters hold [•] per cent in the current paid up and issued share capital of the Company. The shareholding pattern of the Company as on the Effective Date is as set forth in Schedule 1 hereto. |

A start-up has three categories of shareholders in this respect: founders who hold equity, investors who hold equity, and investors who hold convertible securities that have not yet been converted into shares.

A founder needs to ensure that they add the fully diluted cap table here, taking into consideration the securities that will be converted at a future date.

Details on the fully diluted cap table before the investment takes place are added to a document called Schedule 1.

1.4	**Instruments**	Equity shares having a face value of INR [•] each at a price of [•] per share ('Equity Shares'). 'Definitive Documentation' shall have the meaning ascribed to it under Clause 3.1 of this Term Sheet

'Instruments' denotes the instrument through which the investment will take place. It can be equity shares, preference shares, Compulsorily Convertible Preference Shares (CCPS), Compulsory Convertible Debentures (CCDs), convertible notes, etc. We will discuss them in a later section.

1.5	**Valuation**	For the purpose of the Proposed Transaction, the pre-money valuation of the Company is INR [•].

The pre-money valuation of the start-up at which the investor puts money into the business is stated in this section. A point that a founder needs to clarify with the investor is whether they have considered the pre-money or the post-money valuation for the investment.

Normally, pre-money valuation + investment = post-money valuation

But if the discussion between the founders and investors is being based on valuation, without specifying if it's pre-money or post-money may lead to confusion and delay.

Assume that the pre-money valuation of your start-up is Rs 75 crore. With an investment of Rs 25 crore, the post-money valuation will amount to Rs 100 crore. If the investor calculates their shareholding using the post-money valuation, they own a 25 per cent stake in the company. But if there was a miscommunication and the investors meant that Rs 75 crore is to be the post-money valuation after their investment of Rs 25 crore, their shareholding becomes 25/75, or 33 per cent of the company. There's an evident mismatch.

While on the subject, is also important to know how the issuance of shares work, pre and post money. The pie chart below should clarify it.

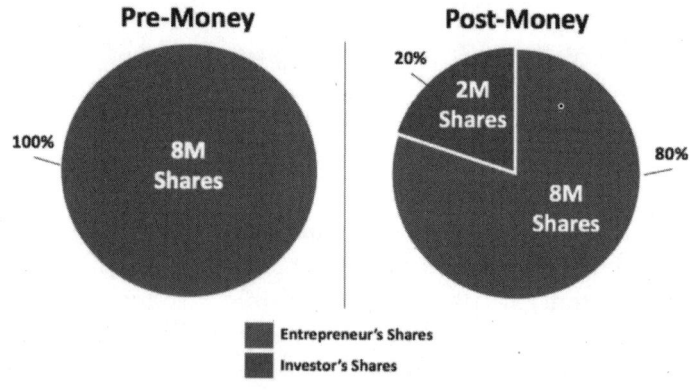

Similarly, if you already have some investors on your cap table and are now inducting new investors, this is how the new share split will pan out:

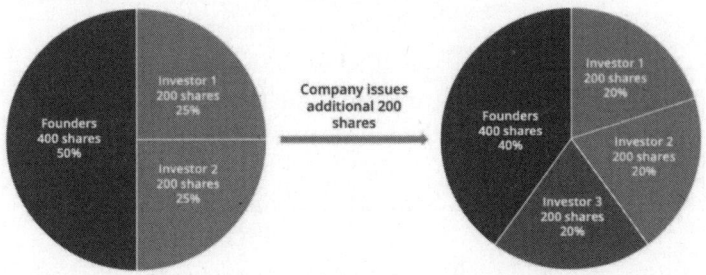

| 1.6 | **Proposed Transaction** | (i) Subject to applicable law, the Investor, along with certain other persons as set forth in the Definitive Documentation (collectively, 'Investors') proposes to make an investment of up to INR [•] (the 'Investment Amount') into the Company such that the post-investment shareholding structure of the Company shall be in the manner set out in Schedule 2 hereunder. It is agreed by the Parties that the Investment Amount may be subject to change at any time subsequent to the execution of this Term Sheet but prior to the execution of the Definitive Documentation, and in the event of the same, the post-money valuation and shareholding pattern of the Company shall be accordingly revised. (ii) The Parties will work towards achieving completion of the |

> Proposed Transaction, including but not limited to the remittance of the Investment Amount and issue of corresponding Equity Shares ('Closing') within the timeframe specified in the SSSHA.
> (iii) The shareholding pattern of the Company, immediately upon Closing, shall be as set forth in Schedule 2 hereunder.

A founder should make sure that the two schedules, Schedule 1 and 2, are clarified and agreed upon during the negotiations to avoid any confusion in the future.

This section also states that the valuation of the company may change during the due diligence, and hence, the shareholding pattern may have to be revised. During due diligence, the investor may find some metrics to be worse than what was initially believed and may insist on reducing the company's valuation on that basis. Hence, they add this statement in their interest.

| 1.7 | **Advisory Equity** | The Company agrees to issue at the time of Closing, to [•], Equity Shares ('Advisory Equity') equivalent to [•] per cent of [•] in value, in consideration of the advisory and mentoring services to be rendered by [•] on an ongoing basis, subject to the terms set forth in the Definitive Documentation. [LV Note: This is an optional clause and is to be included if an investor is getting advisory equity.] |

Advisor equity details the pool of equity set aside for advisers of the start-up and is an optional clause.

Investors generally want founders to issue adviser shares from their own shares so that the investors' holding is not diluted.

Key Considerations

2.1	**Board Composition and Incidental Matters**	The Company is currently engaged in the business of [•]. The Board of Directors of the Company (the 'Board') immediately upon Closing shall comprise of [•] directors, of which the Investors shall be entitled to nominate 1 (one) director ('Investor Director') and the other directors shall be nominated by the Promoters. In the event of any increase or decrease in the number of directors, the number of directors so nominated by the Investors and the Promoters shall be proportionately increased or decreased. The Investors shall be entitled to nominate 1 (one) person as the observer of the proceedings of the Board ('Board Observer').

This is a control term and refers to the demand of investors to appoint a director and/or a board observer. Investors can have two types of control as board members—positive and negative.

Positive control is the investor's ability to vote as a director in the board meetings and shareholders' meetings.

Negative control mean that your business cannot do certain things unless formally approved by investors. These are also known as protective provisions, such as future fundraising, change in shareholding structure, taking debt, merger and acquisition decisions, etc., and are covered as veto rights under the Reserved Matters of the Shareholder's Agreement.

Read and negotiate hard on the negative controls to retain maximum control. What you cannot negotiate to remove, insist on getting a threshold in. For example, if a change in related party transactions would require investor approval, you can negotiate that increase in related party transactions only above Rs 50 lakh per annum requires such approval.

An investor may appoint a board observer who has the right to attend the board meetings of the company. They do not have voting rights but can let their opinions be known.

Investors often take the right to appoint a board observer but rarely do so. Instead of spending time during negotiation on removing the board observer, talk to other founders that the investor has invested in and ask them whether they really appoint a board observer.

You need to understand the motive of your investors well and take an appropriate call on the items you need to spend more time on during negotiations.

2.2	**Pre-emptive Rights**	The Investors shall have a pro rata right to participate in any future issue of shares by the Company to any third party and to retain their shareholding on a fully diluted basis in the Company on the same terms and conditions (including price) as offered to such third party. Circumstances where pre-emptive rights will not be applicable will be detailed in the Definitive Documentation.

Assume that an investor holds a certain stake in your company at present. In future, when you issue more shares to other investors, the present-day investors will get the first right to put in money and retain their shareholding on a fully diluted basis.

2.3	**Anti-Dilution Protection**	If at any time after Closing, the Company issues to any third party, equity shares or instruments convertible to equity shares, at a price per share that is lower than the price paid for the Equity Shares (or their conversion price), then the Investors shall be entitled to antidilution protection on a broad based weighted average basis. In such an event, the Company shall be bound to, and the Promoters shall be bound to cooperate with the Investors and the Company such that, the Company forthwith

> takes all necessary steps to issue additional equity shares to the Investors. Circumstances where anti-dilution protection will not be applicable will be detailed in the Definitive Documentation.

If a start-up performs poorly due to any reason, there's a chance that it gets devalued in future investment rounds. The investors coming on the cap table get shares at a price lower than that of earlier investors.

To protect themselves against any such loss in the future, an investor gets the right to buy more shares in the company at a lower price to increase their stake.

There are two kinds of antidilution: full rachet antidilution and weighted average antidilution.

Full ratchet antidilution provisions are used by early-stage investors to protect their interests in case of a downward valuation by a bigger investor at a later stage. If, say, an investor invests at Rs 10 per share in a start-up, but later, another investor puts in money at Rs 5 per share, that means the start-up's valuation has halved to accommodate the new investor. In such a case, the previous investor's shares would now also be valued at the new price, doubling the equity previously held by the investor, without any new money invested.

In the weighted average antidilution, the number of shares issued at the reduced price is taken into consideration in the repricing of the previous round, and not just the new price flatly. If the number of new shares issued at the reduced price is very low, the older investors don't get any significant advantage because of the low weightage of the new price. Hence, the weighted average anti-dilution is more friendly to start-up founders than rachet-based anti-dilution.

2.4	**Promoters' Lock-in**	The Promoters shall not be entitled to transfer to any person, the shares held by them in the Company, directly or indirectly, for a period of [3 (three)] years from the date of Closing ('Lock-in Period'). The Promoters may however transfer their shares to any person during the Lock-in Period subject to the prior written approval of the Investors and right of first refusal or tag along right as set forth in this Clause 2.

'Promoters' Lock-in' is an economic term and is similar to the concept of ESOPs. Employees get the shares of the company, or exercise their ESOPs gradually as they continue working with the company, depending on the vesting schedule set.

Investors put a lock-in clause on founders to restrict their access to their shares if they stop contributing to the growth of their company.

Similar to the employees, founders receive their shares at the end of each year that they spend with the company or any other defined period. This is also known as reverse vesting. Usually, the period is taken as three to four years if investment happens in the early stages.

If you have spent a considerable time, say three years, already building the company, you can negotiate shorter reverse vesting of, say, one or two years on account of this time invested.

2.5 **Vesting of Promoters' Shares**

25 per cent of the shares held by each Promoter shall be deemed to have vested on the date hereof, and the remaining 75 per cent of the shares held by each Promoter ('Unvested Shares') will be restricted over a 4-year period starting from the date of Closing ('Vesting Period'). Upon the completion of the first year, the Unvested Shares will be vested in equal instalments, every [3 (three)] months, over the next [3 (three)] years and shall cease to be part of the Unvested Shares. It is hereby clarified that the first quarterly vesting shall occur at the end of the 15th (fifteenth) month. In the event of termination of any of the Promoters' employment with the Company any time during the Vesting Period, only the shares that remain part of the Unvested Shares shall be transferred to the Company and in the event such transfer to the Company is not feasible (by reason of restrictions under applicable law or otherwise), such Unvested Shares shall be disposed of in a manner determined by the Board and the Investors.
[LV Note: The manner of disposal of the Unvested Shares can be customized based on the understanding between the Parties.]

This clause gives the details on how the shares of the founders will be vested from year to year. When an investor comes on board, they make the founders earn their shares through the reverse vesting clauses, as stated in the previous section.

But what happens if the investors fire the founder and replace them with another CEO? If it happens at the end of two years of a four-year reverse vesting period, the founder will hold only 50 per cent of their actual shares, as only 2/4 of their shareholding would have been vested. However, if the founder has the accelerated vesting clause put in the Shareholder's Agreement, it will ensure that if they are terminated without cause (i.e., for reasons other than fraud), their unvested shares will immediately stand vested.

It must be noted that a founder may not want accelerated vesting for all of their top management, because it, in a way, incentivizes getting fired without cause and still getting to earn their entire shareholding through accelerated vesting.

2.6	**Promoters' and Non-Selling Investors' Right of First Offer**	In the event any of the Investors ('Selling Investor') intends to sell all or part of their shareholding ('ROFO Shares') in the Company to a third party ('Third Party Buyer'), then such Selling Investor shall first offer to sell the same to the Promoters and in the event: (a) the Promoters refuse to purchase the same; or (b) such Selling Investor obtains an offer from any Investor other than the Selling Investor ('Non-Selling Investor') for purchase of the ROFO Shares at a price higher than the price at which the

> same was offered to be purchased by the Promoters ('Offer Price'), then such Selling Investor shall sell the ROFO Shares to such Non-Selling Investor, provided that the price of the ROFO Shares shall not be lower than the Offer Price.
>
> The Promoters and the Non-Selling Investors shall each have the right to purchase the ROFO Shares in proportion of their respective shareholding in the Company at the Offer Price (or higher).
>
> In the event: (a) none of the Non-Selling Investors agree to purchase the ROFO Shares; or (b) the Selling Investor obtains an offer from a Third Party Buyer for purchase of the ROFO Shares at a price higher than the Offer Price, then such Selling Investor shall sell such ROFO Shares to such Third Party Buyer, provided that the price of the ROFO Shares shall not be lower than the Offer Price.

Every investor, at some point, wants to earn their profits and take an exit. For whatever reason, if an investor wants an exit and starts finding suitors in the market to sell their shares, a negative sentiment against the start-up may develop in the ecosystem. It sends a signal that things are probably not well so the investor wants out.

A founder wishes to avoid this scenario. ROFO ensures that if an investor wants to sell their shares, they must approach the founders first.

If the investor has asked for a higher price, the founder may not be able to afford to buy all their shares. But they can agree to a purchase by a different investor that they bring in because a higher price also means a higher valuation and hence, a positive signal to the market.

In case the price is lower, the founder can take some time and either purchase the shares on their own or manage the transaction internally with the help of other investors of the company. If the deal occurs within a start-up, the news can be controlled with no damage to perception.

A founder should always ask for ROFO rights in the Term Sheet.

2.7	**Investors' Right of First Refusal**	Subject to the Promoter's lock-in as set forth in Clause 2.4 of this Term Sheet, in the event any of the Promoters or any shareholders other than the Investors ('Selling Shareholder') intends to sell all or part of their shareholding ('ROFR Shares') in the Company to any person, then such Selling Shareholder(s) shall first offer the ROFR Shares, to all the Investors ('Non-Selling Shareholders') at the same price as they have offered to such person. The Non-Selling Shareholders, at their sole discretion, shall have the right to purchase the ROFR Shares in proportion to their inter se shareholding in the Company.

Now if a founder wants to sell their shares of the company, ROFR ensures that the first offer to purchase the shares needs to be made to the existing investors of the start-up. Only when the investors refuse to purchase the shares, can the founders sell their stake to third-party investors. Their refusal, however, develops a perception among the other investors that the shares may be overvalued.

ROFR is usually a measure that investors take to dissuade external investors from buying the shares of the founders.

| 2.8 | **Tag-Along Right** | Subject to the Promoter's lock-in as set for in Clause 2.4 of this Term Sheet, in the event any of the Promoters, or the other shareholders other than the Investors decide to sell their shareholding in the Company or a portion of it to any person ('Buyer'), and the Investors do not exercise their right of first refusal as referred to under Clause 2.7 of this Term Sheet, then the Investors shall have the right (but not the obligation) to require the Promoters or the other shareholders as the case may be, to ensure that the Buyer purchases the pro-rata Equity Shares on the same terms and simultaneously with the shares of the Promoters and the other shareholders. The Promoters and/or the other shareholders shall not sell any of their shares to the Buyer unless the Buyer purchases the Equity Shares. It is hereby clarified that any transfer of shares by any of the Investors shall not be subject to any tag-along rights. The procedure governing exercise of tag-along right will be detailed in the Definitive Documentation. |

These rights allow an investor or shareholder (including the founders) to tag along with another bigger shareholder, who may be negotiating a deal of sale of his shares in the company. This means that the new buyer of shares may have to purchase shares of not just the shareholder negotiating the deal, but of every other shareholder who has tag-along rights.

If the founder seeks an exit from the start-up, it becomes especially mandatory for them to get their investors an exit as well. Tag-along rights are a control term that investors impose over founders to restrict their capacity of selling shares of the start-up.

2.9	**ESOP**	The Company shall implement an Employee Stock Option Plan ('ESOP') constituting at least [•] per cent and not exceeding [•] per cent of the post-issue share capital of the Company on a fully diluted basis, with approval of the Investor Director, the quantum of which will be decided in the Definitive Documentation. The ESOP will be used for attracting and retaining talent in the Company.

ESOPs are stock options given to employees to award them for their efforts in building the start-up. Similar to the adviser equity, the investor will ask the founders to set aside an ESOP pool before they enter the cap table. This means that the investor will not be diluted but only the founders will be diluted by the equity set aside for ESOPs. Hence, it is an economic term and you will have to negotiate that the ESOP pool is implemented post the issues of the investor's shares.

Investors may also ask a founder to set aside a standard 10 per cent or 20 per cent of the equity as an unissued ESOP pool. Unless the founders clearly see the need to set aside a large ESOP pool, they will have to negotiate and justify a smaller pool to reduce their dilution.

A few points that founders, depending on their situation, can use to negotiate:

- If all key people are already a part of the founding team, there's no need of setting aside a large ESOP pool
- Number of potential hires may be low
- Number of key personnel required may be low

There can be many other pointers, but it's imperative to have sound reasoning to build your case for a lower ESOP pool. At no point should it appear that your individual wants are above the company's priorities.

| 2.10 | **Affirmative Voting Rights** | The Company and its shareholders shall not be permitted to take any decisions on certain matters without such matters having first received the approval of the Investor Director at a Board meeting. The customary affirmative rights will be listed in the Definitive Documentation. The Investors will have the right to vote pro-rata to their shareholding (on an as if converted basis) in all shareholder meetings. |

The voting rights are based on the powers the investors hold through seats on the board of directors' table. It details the instances when the founders need the approval of the investors to move forward with decisions and when they do not.

2.11	**Liquidation Preference**	Subject to applicable law, the holders of Equity Shares shall have preference over other equity shareholders ('Liquidation Preference') to distribution from the Company or from other third parties, as the case may be, upon the occurrence of a liquidation event (as described in the Definitive Documentation) and shall be entitled to receive in preference to the holders of other equity shares, an amount which is equal to either: (a) the pro-rata share of the Investor's shareholding on as if converted basis plus all declared but unpaid dividends; or (b) the Investment Amount plus all declared but unpaid dividends, whichever is higher. Transactions constituting liquidation event shall be detailed in the Definitive Documentation.

Liquidation preference occurs in two manners: Participating and Non-participating. In Section Six, 'Fundraising Instruments and Mechanics', we'll see how founders are at a disadvantage when participating preference shares are issued to investors.

Negotiate for investors to receive non-participating shares, or at least get scenarios built in to ensure that as a founder, you are not at a complete disadvantage while still covering investors' apprehensions.

2.12	**Information Rights**	As long as the Investors hold any shares in the Company, the Investors shall receive from the Company (i) quarterly (un-audited) financial statements within [30 (thirty)] calendar days from the end of the preceding quarter, (ii) annual (audited) financial statements within [60 (sixty)] calendar days following the closure of the preceding financial year, (iii) operating / business plan within [30 (thirty)] calendar days prior to the commencement of the following year and (iv) any other operational and financial information as per the requirement of the Investors.

When an investor puts money into a start-up, it is natural that they want to stay informed on the progress of the business. They include this clause in the Term Sheet stating the information they seek and at what frequency.

A founder should try to negotiate and minimize the frequency of this information-sharing. It takes effort to prepare such reports and it shouldn't lead them to keep a dedicated resource just for this purpose.

| 2.13 | **Exit Mechanism** | 1. The Company and the Promoters shall make all reasonable endeavours to provide exit to the Investors by way of: (a) an initial public offering of the Company at a mutually agreed minimum valuation within 5 (five) years from the date of Closing; or (b) strategic sale of the Equity Shares at the price acceptable to the Investors within 6 (six) years from the date of Closing provided the Company and the Promoters fail to facilitate an exit under Clause 2.13(1)(a) above.
2. Drag Along Option: In the event the Company and the Promoters fail to provide an exit to the Investors in accordance with Clause 2.13(1) above, the Investors shall have the unilateral right to sell their Investor Instruments (including shares) to any third party and the right to drag along the Promoters requiring the Promoters to sell whole or part of their shares, if required by such third party, to enable exit by the Investors. |
|---|---|---|

> Detailed provisions with respect to the exit rights of the Investors shall be incorporated under the Definitive Documentation.

The founder is duty-bound to provide a successful and profitable exit to their investors. This exit usually takes place as an IPO, strategic sale or drag along option.

An IPO is the liquidation event when a company goes public and lists on the stock markets. A strategic sale may take place in the form of an acquisition by a larger business.

Drag along options are a control term that the investors hold. If investors feel that the founders are driving the company's value down or there is not much growth potential any more, the investors can find a prospective buyer for their shares and get them to buy the entire company. This can be done when they have the right to drag along every other shareholder to compulsorily sell to the prospective buyer at the terms negotiated.

| 2.14 | **Free Transferability** | Subject to Clause 2.6 and provided that the Investors do not sell the Company's securities held by them to any competitor of the Company, the securities held by the Investors in the Company shall be freely transferable at any point of time, subject to applicable law. The term 'competitor' shall be defined in the Definitive Documentation. |

This clause builds on the ROFO rights and states that the investors are allowed to sell their shares based on the terms and conditions that have been stated in the Term Sheet.

4.0 General

4.1	**Expenses**	All costs and expenses which constitute the basic and requisite transactional expenses in respect of the transaction contemplated herein (including consultancy/advisory fees, due diligence, stamp duty or other statutory charges) ('Basic Expenses') shall be borne by the Company. Any expense in addition to the Basic Expenses initiated by an Investor shall be borne by such Investor.

It has become an industry standard that the start-up has to pay all the professional charges incurred in the process of raising funds, both on their and the investors' sides.

You can negotiate to put a cap on the lawyer's fees. Lawyers usually charge on an hourly basis, and without constraints, they may take longer to draft the agreements leading to higher costs.

4.2	**Confidentiality**	Each party hereto shall keep all information about the Proposed Transaction (including the terms of this Term Sheet and the discussions between the parties) confidential and shall not disclose the same to any

third party without the prior written approval of the other parties. Standard exceptions to confidentiality obligations (including disclosure of information mandated under applicable law) shall apply. Any disclosure to a party's representatives, employees, agents or assigns shall be strictly on a need-to-know basis.

Investors include this clause of confidentiality to prevent the founders from term sheet shopping. So, when you negotiate with other investors for a deal, you must be careful about the information you disclose. This clause is binding and the investors can take legal action if you disclose details about their offer externally.

4.3	**Exclusivity**	The Company and the Promoters agree that following [60 (sixty)] days from the execution of this Term Sheet, neither the Promoters nor the Company, either by themselves or through any other person, shall approach or participate in any discussions or negotiations or solicit, discuss and/or encourage any financing for the Company by any other person in any manner and will not provide any information relating to the Company to any other potential investor and will clearly indicate to such other potential investors that the Company and the Promoters are bound by this Clause 4.3.

This clause is another protective measure investors take to dissuade founders from negotiating deals with other investors. It states that the Term Sheet and the offer of investment are exclusive and the founder cannot discuss the details with any other potential investor.

4.4	**Termination**	This Term Sheet shall terminate [90 (ninety)] days from its execution unless mutually extended by the parties or mutually cancelled by the parties. It shall automatically stand terminated upon replacement by the Definitive Documentation.

A term sheet stands valid for a certain number of days, usually ninety. Unless this duration is mutually extended by both the parties, the offer will stand cancelled after the period is over. The term sheet is automatically terminated and replaced by the Definitive Documents upon their signing.

4.5	**Amendment**	The parties may amend the terms of this Term Sheet by mutual consent in writing.

The amendment clause is self-explanatory and states that the terms of the term sheet can be changed by getting mutual consent from the investors and the founders.

The term sheet is governed by the laws of India.

A founder must ensure that the jurisdiction is set as the state in which the company is registered. If set in the investor's state, then if things go wrong and you face a legal suit, you will have to spend additional time and money travelling to that location.

Classifying Term Sheet Clauses

Every founder should prepare to negotiate the clauses of the term sheet and place them in the start-up's favour as much as possible. A thinking framework to proceed with this preparation is to divide the clauses into three categories as follows.

1. **Non-negotiable**: These are those clauses or terms that you consider non-negotiable. If these are not fulfilled, then you'll strongly consider backing out from the association.
2. **Negotiable**: These are the clauses that you will try and make more favourable for yourself but are ready to compromise to some extent. Having a priority order of the clauses more critical to you would help with better planning.
3. **Leverage**: Always have a set of clauses that you can use as leverage to negotiate for better terms elsewhere. These may be otherwise acceptable to you in their current form, but the investors may not be sure of that. You can use this gap in knowledge to negotiate better terms on the non-negotiable and negotiable clauses.

BATNA and the Need for Multiple Investors

BATNA stands for Best Alternative to a Negotiated Agreement and refers to the bargaining power you gain when there are multiple investors interested in your start-up. When you have multiple interested parties, it allows you to compare the offers made. When an offer is in hand, the BATNA is simply the best alternative to it, and it gives you more bargaining power to negotiate with either of the investors.

Needless to say, however, that you must always stay within the confines of professionalism and not go overboard with term sheet shopping. The investor community is tight-knit and knowledge about your negotiations with multiple investors is likely to spread quickly. The other aspect that you need to be very careful about is not to disclose the details of any term sheet. The confidentiality clause of the term sheet, as stated earlier, is legally binding.

Timelines

Once you receive the term sheet, remember that if all goes well, it takes another 1 to 1.5 months for the due diligence to take place. The more advanced the stage, the longer this process takes. Finally, it takes another 1 to 1.5 months at least to complete all the compliance-related paperwork. These are sequential in nature, and many filings can happen only after the previous one has concluded. If any part of the process becomes a bottleneck, it elongates the conclusion further.

You can safely assume that it would take three months or more for the money to hit the bank account after receiving the term sheet. If there are any irregularities found between your claims and actuals, the process may take much longer.

Should You Get an Investment Banker?

To execute a fundraising round, you basically need three types of people. A CFO or a CFO-equivalent who can take charge of the entire process on the start-up's behalf. A financial adviser, usually a CA experienced in this industry and on such deals, who helps ascertain a valuation. Then there's someone to manage the legal compliances and paperwork, usually a CS or a lawyer experienced in this domain.

In the early stages, the requirements are lower. Since there's not a lot of data or history to study, due diligence is faster. As long as there's a representative from the company (could be one of the founders) to assist in basic requirements, the process can be concluded smoothly even without an investment banker. However, I do advise getting a start-up legal expert (not any legal expert) to help founders study the term sheet and avoid any unnecessary pitfalls. Incubators and accelerators usually provide their start-ups with such assistance in executing the round.

Having said this, fundraising is indeed a time-consuming process and many founders would prefer to spend their time working on the core business. If there's a CFO on the team, they can undertake this responsibility, but if not, getting an investment banker will help them save a lot of time and effort.

In the later stages though, getting an investment banker becomes a necessity. Unless you have a highly capable CFO experienced in executing funding rounds earlier, it would be incredibly hard to do it without one.

* * *

Start-up India Seed Fund Scheme

Just as we close this section on the brass tacks of funding, I thought it would be the right place to discuss one more source of early-stage start-up investments, namely, the Start-up India Seed Fund Scheme (SISFS). Ever so often, one encounters some amount of scepticism with regard to how easy it will be to receive funding via a government scheme. It will be worthwhile therefore to present some statistics at the outset. As of 31 May, 2024, as many as 217 incubators have been selected under the scheme and a total of

Rs 841 crore was disbursed to them. The number of start-ups who have been selected, as of the same date, stand at 2235 and the amount disbursed stands at Rs 386 crore.

Under the scheme, a start-up is eligible to receive seed funding as below:

- Up to Rs 20 lakh as grant for validation of Proof of Concept or prototype development or product trials. The grant shall be disbursed in milestone-based instalments related to development of prototype, product testing, building a product ready for market launch, etc.
- Up to Rs 50 lakh of investment for market entry, commercialization or scaling up through convertible or debt or debt-linked instruments.

The eligibility criteria for the scheme are as below:

- A start-up recognized by the Department for Promotion of Industry and Internal Trade (DPIIT), incorporated not more than two years ago at the time of application.
- The start-up should be using technology in its core product or service or business model or distribution model or methodology to solve the problem being targeted.
- Preference would be given to start-ups creating innovative solutions in sectors such as social impact, waste management, water management, financial inclusion, education, agriculture, food processing, biotechnology, healthcare, energy, mobility, defence, space, railways, oil and gas, and textiles.
- A start-up applicant can avail seed support in the form of grant and debt/convertible debentures each once as per the guidelines of the scheme.

In applying for the scheme, the start-ups are required to fill a form where they need to detail aspects such as the problem they are solving, their value proposition, the need for the idea, potential impact, fund utilization plan, among others.

Pro-tip: The form also requires you to fill your choice of top three incubators. Before you do that, be sure to look at the state-wise breakdown of incubators that is available under the scheme. The website details the total amount approved to them as well as the total funds disbursed. It will be worthwhile to make a choice of incubators carefully, taking into account the amounts that are available with them for disbursement. The mistake start-ups often make is to go with popular incubators without taking this aspect into account and lose out in the process.

Section Six

Getting the Deal Through

- Due Diligence
- Fundraising Instruments and Mechanics
- Fundraising Paperwork and Compliance

In the previous section, we discussed the broad mechanics of a term sheet. While a term sheet may be perceived as the end of the fundraising journey for a particular round, it is actually only the beginning. In this section, let us run through the many aspects involved in the fundraising process after a term sheet is signed.

To give you a broad overview of the aspects involved, let me begin by sharing with you a handy spreadsheet that I often use with my clients during the fundraising process. Not only does it list the various steps involved, in this case, it also fixes responsibility for each of the steps by identifying the single point of contact.

	Action Points	SPOC
1	Draft Term Sheet	Sarthak
2	Discuss and close Term Sheet with Angel Representative - Choose between ABC / XYZ - Negotiate with them and get signed approval - Float Term Sheet among angels and get written approval on email - Collect Investors' KYC (PAN, Aadhaar, Bank Account details)	Founder 1
3	Draft SSHA	Sarthak
4	Amendment of MoA for Authorized Capital - Increase Authorized Capital for 3,000 "Pre-Seed CCPS" of Rs. 10 each - Minutes of Board Meeting calling EGM - Notice & Explanatory Statement of EGM - Minutes of EGM - File Form MGT-14 - File Form SH-7	Kashika
5	Negotiate the SSHA with the lawyer of Angel Rep	Sarthak & Founder 1
6	Registered Valuer's Certificate (Assuming all angels are Resident)	Kashika
7	Opening of a "Share Application Money" bank account	Founder 1
8	Issuance of Shares - Minutes of Board Meeting calling EGM - Notice & Explanatory Statement of EGM - Minutes of EGM - Draft PAS-4 and float among all investors - File Form MGT-14	Kashika
8	Issuance of Shares - Minutes of Board Meeting calling EGM - Notice & Explanatory Statement of EGM - Minutes of EGM - Draft PAS-4 and float among all investors - File Form MGT-14	Kashika
9	Call Money and Coordinate with all Angels	Founder 1
10	Procure Stamp Papers for SSHA, etc	Kashika
11	File Form PAS-3 on MCA for allotment of shares	Kashika
12	Create Share Certificates and send them to all Angels	Kashika
13	Apply for Payment of Stamp Duty on Share Certificates	Kashika
14	Amendment of AoA to incorporate SSHA Terms - Minutes of Board Meeting calling EGM - Notice & Explanatory Statement of EGM - Minutes of EGM - File Form MGT-14	Kashika

Due Diligence

While the term sheet is, at best, a principal agreement to invest the money, it finally goes through only after investors thoroughly study the company and corroborate the claims made by the founders. Due diligence is typically known to take three forms:

- Financial (FDD)
- Legal (LDD)
- Technical (TDD)

Let us run through each of them to understand what they entail.

Financial Due Diligence (FDD)

The goal with this due diligence is to verify the financial numbers claimed by the founders in their pitch deck. Essentially, all the financial metrics critical to the health of your start-up are analysed and discrepancies, if any, called out.

Take for instance, a start-up—let us call it 'Company A'—had claimed a certain sales figure as their revenue number. While in many cases the sales and revenue figures are interchangeable, in the case of Company A, the due diligence revealed that the business was selling through an e-commerce website and that the transaction costs had not been factored in while reporting revenues.

As another example, the quality of revenue of the company is analysed and in case the revenue is achieved after offering heavy discounts or by incurring high marketing spends, it is called into question.

Some of the areas of focus of a financial due diligence include:

1. **Historical Financial Performance**
    o Trends in revenue, profitability and expenses

- Identification of one-time or non-recurring items that may distort financial results
2. **Quality of Earnings**
    - Assessing whether reported earnings are sustainable
    - Identifying reliance on one-time gains or unusual accounting practices
3. **Working Capital and Cash Flow**
    - Analysing cash flow stability and liquidity
    - Identifying potential cash flow issues, such as delayed receivables or high inventory levels
4. **Debt and Liabilities**
    - Reviewing outstanding debts and repayment terms
    - Identifying contingent liabilities, such as pending lawsuits or tax disputes
5. **Revenue Sources and Customer Base**
    - Evaluating the diversity of revenue streams
    - Highlighting risks, such as over-reliance on a single customer or market
6. **Internal Controls and Processes**
    - Assessing the adequacy of financial reporting systems
    - Identifying weaknesses in internal controls that could lead to errors or fraud
7. **Tax Compliance**
    - Reviewing tax filings and liabilities
    - Identifying potential risks, such as underpayment or disputes with tax authorities
8. **Forecasts and Projections**
    - Evaluating the reasonableness of financial projections
    - Identifying overly optimistic assumptions or gaps in planning

9. **Industry Benchmarks**
   o Comparing the company's performance to industry peers
   o Highlighting areas of underperformance or competitive advantage

These insights help buyers or investors make informed decisions, mitigate risks and negotiate fair terms.

Legal Due Diligence (LDD)

This involves a thorough review of the company's legal documents and information to assess potential risks and liabilities. It typically includes an assessment of the following aspects:

- Company registration documents
- Legal compliance with various laws, regulations and government mandates
- Examining key contracts and agreements
- Assessing the company's IP assets
- Regulatory compliance
- Any ongoing litigation

Technical Due Diligence (TDD)

As its name suggests, TDD is a comprehensive examination of a company's technology, infrastructure and practices, including its products, software and IT systems. Any gaps in security, capability or data privacy are highlighted here. Some of the aspects covered under TDD include:

- Product and software
- Software and hardware architecture
- Adequacy of IT infrastructure

- Security protocols
- Processes and practices
- Scalability and maintainability
- Code quality
- APIs and integration
- Deployment and hosting
- Cybersecurity

In essence, TDD aims to identify potential issues, evaluate alignment with business goals, assess future growth potential and, of course, provide an informed decision-making framework. It is worth a mention here that the priority areas of this diligence vary by stages. At the seed stage, for instance, the due diligence is likely to focus on the ability to release a competent product. While at Series C, the emphasis is more on the ability to handle high volumes.

Apart from the due diligences mentioned above, some other diligences may also be required depending on the nature of the company and its maturity. Some of these include:

- **Data and Privacy**: For companies such as fintech start-ups that have sensitive customer information, evaluating this aspect is key.
- **User Diligence**: For companies that rely on their user base to generate revenues, ascertaining whether or not their users are real is important. Elon Musk, for instance, had backed out of his $44 billion deal to acquire Twitter in July 2022, on the grounds that the platform had a sizeable number of fake users. He had asserted that Twitter failed to provide sufficient data to verify its claim that less than 5 per cent of its users were fake.
- **Environment, Social, and Governance (ESG)**: It refers to a framework used to evaluate an organization's impact on the environment, its social responsibilities and its

governance practices. ESG is often used by investors to assess the sustainability and ethical impact of their investments. It has gained significant traction in recent years as businesses and stakeholders increasingly prioritize sustainability and social responsibility.

Due Diligence Best Practices

- As a founder, it is imperative that you preschedule daily meetings with internal stakeholders responsible for sharing information with investors. Since due diligence isn't a core business activity, it is unlikely to get concluded quickly, but for your single-minded focus. An activity chart, with specific points of contact, which I shared before, could come in handy.
- Ever so often, internal stakeholders may assume that they have all the information available; however, when the due diligence formats actually hit them, many cracks may surface. Keep a mental buffer for this. To ease the process, I have added to the annexures a handy checklist for the different due diligences.
- Build a comprehensive data room on Google Drive or OneDrive, for easy access to data. Ensure that the editing rights of the same are with one or two people only, to maintain the sanctity of the data.

What If the Due Diligence Does Not Go as Expected?

Needless to say, if the claimed metrics do not match the actuals as unearthed in the process of due diligence, it can lead to a revised valuation or even withdrawal of the investor from the deal.

Particularly, if the discrepancies are seen as a deliberate attempt to deceive the investor, it will indicate dishonesty on the founder's part and will lead to broken trust and a bad name.

In recent times, where we have been swamped with stories of financial irregularities in the start-up space, it only drives up the need of investors to undertake robust due diligence.

Fundraising Instruments and Mechanics

Contrary to the general perception, a founder can raise funds through the use of a number of instruments. Judgement applied in the choice of the right instruments can, in fact, enable founders to protect a large chunk of their equity while still fulfilling their business goals. Let us look at some of these instruments:

a. Understanding Shares—Equity and Preference

Shares, as most of us know, are the units of equity ownership in a company. The value and the ownership stake of any individual or entity in a company depends on the number of shares they hold and the price of each share. All shares, when put together, comprise 100 per cent of the company ownership. In the beginning, when a start-up is just incorporated, the founders hold all these shares among themselves. Gradually, with external investors, the shareholding gets distributed among different stakeholders. We saw an example of the changing shareholding pattern post a fundraise, while we were discussing the elements of the term sheet.

There are primarily two types of shares—equity and preference. Let's understand each of them briefly.

i. Equity shares

Equity shares, also known as ordinary shares, are normally the shares held by founders and employees of the company.

You may be holding equity shares of several companies listed in the stock market. If the company does well, its share price increases and you can opt to sell your shares to make a profit. These equity shares are, evidently, valuable assets that show up in your financial portfolio. However, you obtain a monetary benefit only when these shares are sold and encashed, or the company you hold the shares of decides to pay a dividend.

With start-ups, equity shares or any type of shares, for that matter, cannot be traded publicly. These are relatively illiquid and instances of sale of shares occur under very controlled settings. However, if the company does get acquired for a large amount, these equity shareholders enjoy the upside that comes with it.

Equity investing in start-ups, however, is also inherently risky. There are ways, therefore, through which investors safeguard their interests. One of them is through preference shares.

ii. Preference Shares

Preference shares, also known as preferred stock, are a type of company share that give their holders priority over ordinary shareholders in a liquidation event. A liquidation event, in most cases, refers to an acquisition by a larger organization or a private purchase of a company's shares by another investor.

Conventionally, preference shares are also a medium to prioritize the dividend payout for such shareholders. That is, if a company creates an annual dividend pool, it is the holders of preference shares that get the dividend first. However, when such shares are allotted, this dividend rate is capped. For example, issuing 10 per cent preference shares means the shareholder is entitled to annually receive a 10 per cent dividend on the face value of the shares they hold, and this payout will be prioritized over the dividends of the equity shareholders.

Let us try and summarize some of the key differences between equity and preference shares:

	Equity	**Preference**
Purpose	Owner	First Claim on Profits
Risk	Highest	Lower than Equity
Upside	Highest	Fixed
Expectation	Capital Gain	Dividends
Repayment	Last on Liquidation	Before Equity Shareholders

	Equity	**Preference**
Voting Rights	Yes	No
Bonus Shares	Eligible	Not Eligible
Redemption	Not Allowed	Redeemable
Investor Type	Long Term	Medium Term
Dividend Arrears	Mostly Not	Eligible for Arrears

You will notice how holding each of these shares comes with their own individual benefits. As an investor, however, you want to achieve the benefits of both—you want your principal to be protected while you also want a stake in surplus profits.

An example should make this clearer. Say a start-up raises funding of Rs 2 crore at a valuation of Rs 10 crore. In effect, it means that the start-up is selling 20 per cent of its equity to the investor while the founder retains 80 per cent ownership.

Now, let us go on to assume that a year later, the same start-up gets acquired for Rs 5 crore. In this eventuality, how much does the founder get and what is the investor's share?

A simple calculation will show that the investor gets 20 per cent of Rs 5 crore which is Rs 1 crore and the founder gets as much as Rs 4 crore. Considering that the investor had pumped in funding worth Rs 2 crore, this clearly puts the investor at a disadvantage. To protect themselves from such a scenario, investors want to have what is known as a liquidation preference. In the above case, if the investor had a 1x liquidation preference, that would have entitled them to receive the amount they had invested, namely, Rs 2 crore. In this case, the founder then would get the remaining Rs 3 crore. So far so good.

Now, let us take an alternate scenario in which the start-up gets acquired for Rs 20 crore as opposed to Rs 5 crore in the previous example. Even if the investor has a 1x liquidation preference, it would still fetch the investor only Rs 2 crore while the founder would get the remaining Rs 18 crore. Clearly, not a desirable situation for the investor.

In order to both protect their principal and get an upside on profits, investors like to invest through a hybrid instrument called Compulsorily Convertible Preference Shares (CCPS). A CCPS is a subtype of an investment instrument known as a convertible security. We will soon get into its mechanics. Before doing that, let us just answer one question.

Can an Investor Invest Without a Valuation?

While typically we associate the funding process as subsequent to arriving at a valuation of the business, the fact is start-ups also get funded at stages where there is no clear indication of how the business will shape up. The key financial metrics that are evaluated aren't available at this point. In such cases, unvalued rounds are often the norm. In these cases, the valuation is deferred to a later stage when the start-up generates enough traction. Investors who invest in early rounds without a proper valuation get the benefit of a valuation discount or a valuation cap. Simply put, a valuation discount means that early investors get a predetermined discount on the share price after valuation. A valuation cap, on the other hand, guarantees a certain minimum stake to the early investor. The valuation cap is the highest valuation at which shares are allocated to early investors.

Below is a quick summary of the primary differences between a valued versus unvalued round:

Parameters	Valued	Unvalued
Stage of investment	Series A and beyond	Pre-seed and seed
Amount of investment	Upwards of $500,000	$100,000–1 million
Type of investor	Marquee VC firms	Angel investors, incubators, accelerators, micro VC firms
Use of funds	Scale products and increase revenue	MVP and initial users

Parameters	Valued	Unvalued
Instruments used	CCPS, Equity	CN, CCD
Time to conclude	3–6 months	1–2 months

* CCPS = Compulsorily Convertible Preference Shares
* CN = Convertible Note
* CCD = Compulsorily Convertible Debentures

That question answered, let us now get into the mechanics of the hybrid instruments.

Convertible Securities

Convertible securities combine features of both debt and equity, offering flexibility to investors and a cost-effective way for companies to raise capital.

As the name suggests, a convertible security is an investment instrument that can be changed from one form to another based on certain conditions. The way that it typically works is that it starts out in the form of debt and then gets converted to equity, either at a conversion event or when the maturity period is over.

A conversion event is defined as the point in time when the investment turns into equity. It is defined in the agreement signed by the start-up and the investors. An example of a conversion event may look like this:

'The convertible security of Rs 1 crore will convert to equity when the start-up raises an investment of at least Rs 10 crore at a valuation of at most Rs 100 crore in a future round.'

Convertible securities come with a floor and a cap. The floor is the minimum future valuation at which the convertible security will convert to equity, and the cap is the corresponding maximum valuation. These numbers depend on the expected fundraising amount in the subsequent rounds.

Convertible securities often also include a discount on the conversion. It is a method to reward early investors of the business for the higher risk they took on their investment. Instead of allocating them shares at the current fair price, they are given the allocated shares at a discount; thus they get a relatively larger portion of the company compared to other investors who come in late. Typically, the standard rate of discount offered in convertible securities is 20 per cent. A share with a face value of Rs 100 is thus offered at a cost of Rs 80 at the time of conversion.

Based on the features and uses, convertible securities can, in turn, be categorized into three types:

1. Convertible Note (CN)
2. Compulsorily Convertible Preference Shares (CCPS)
3. Compulsorily Convertible Debentures (CCD)

Convertible Notes (CN)

A convertible note (CN) is a debt instrument issued in the form of a simple loan agreement that converts to equity typically in a subsequent valued financing round. It is often used by start-ups in the seed or pre-seed stages when valuing the company may not be straightforward. It's also executed in a relatively shorter time, making it favourable for early-stage founders.

Since convertible notes are mainly employed by early investors of a start-up, their investment is converted into shares at a discounted rate to reward them for the higher risk that they took. The discount can be given either as a flat 20 per cent discount on the price or as a valuation cap.

Here is a quick summary of the key differences between a convertible note and equity:

Convertible notes vs. Equity

ASPECT	CONVERTIBLE NOTES	EQUITY FUNDRAISING
Nature	Short-term debt that can convert into equity	Direct ownership in the company through shares
Valuation	Doesn't require immediate company valuation	Requires company valuation
Hussle	Easier and faster due to less negotiation and documentation	Slower due to more thorough due diligence and legal complexity
Investor Control	Little-to-no voting rights or control until conversion	Often includes voting rights, control, and information rights

waveup.com

It is important to note that convertible notes require a minimum investment of Rs 25 lakh. Also, the start-up being invested in should be registered on the Start-up India website under DPIIT.

SAFE and iSAFE

Y Combinator developed SAFE back in 2013 as a type of convertible note. SAFE stands for Simple Agreement for Future Equity and is a form of convertible security issued by early-stage start-ups to raise funds in their initial round.

SAFE notes can be converted to equity shares at the next valuation round at a discount. They are inexpensive and fast to execute. A start-up can raise funds through SAFE in less than a month at a cost of approximately Rs 30,000 in professional fees.

However, SAFE is not an instrument available to start-ups incorporated in India. Here, 100X.VC popularized iSAFE, or India SAFE, as an Indian equivalent of SAFE. The iSAFE document can be downloaded from the 100X.VC website.

It works quite like the convertible note we read about.

b. Compulsorily Convertible Preference Shares

Investors are known to invest in start-ups through an instrument called Compulsorily Convertible Preference Shares (CCPS), which gives them the benefit of protection of their principal as well as a stake in surplus profits.

CCPS are preference shares allotted to investors that must convert to equity shares after a predetermined period or on achieving predefined milestones. Usually, this conversion happens when the investor wants an exit after making a substantial profit on their investment. Essentially, CCPS allows the investor to enjoy a preference in a liquidation event over the equity shareholders, as well as claim a stake in the profits.

For the amount invested, investors get the commensurate number of shares based on the share price. Additionally, they can be given a certain liquidation preference, e.g. 1x, 1.5x, 2x, etc. This means that during a liquidation event, these shareholders will have the first right to encash a certain multiple of the principal invested. In a 2x liquidation preference, for instance, preference shareholders have the right to claim double the principal they invested before the surplus gets shared among the equity shareholders.

There's also the concept of participating and non-participating liquidation preference. Let's understand these through an example.

Example 1: 10 per cent CCPS at 1x participating liquidity preference

Assume a start-up has raised a seed round in equity funding. An investor invests Rs 2 crore in the start-up at a valuation of Rs 10 crore for a 20 per cent stake. The investor has been allotted CCPS with a dividend cap of 10 per cent and a 1x participating liquidation preference.

At the end of year 1, the investors are entitled to receive Rs 20 lakh (10 per cent of Rs 2 crore) as a dividend.

At the end of year 2, they receive an additional Rs 20 lakh as stipulated.

The dividends can either be paid out every year or continue accumulating each year as returns until they hold these shares. This means that at the end of year 2, their investment of Rs 2 crore has grown to Rs 2.4 crore through dividends.

Let's say the start-up gets an acquisition offer of Rs 15 crore at this point.

Since the investors hold preference shares and have a 1x liquidation preference, they get the first right to encash their investment in the company. The investors will receive Rs 2.4 crore out of the total Rs 15 crore as a return on their investment.

Now, since they have a 'participating' liquidation preference, it means that the investors can participate in the residual profits as well.

Apart from claiming the 1x liquidation as preference shareholders, they can also convert these to equity shares and partake in the surplus profits left after pocketing their Rs 2.4 crore, which is Rs 12.6 crore.

After converting their preference shares to equity shares, since they hold a 20 per cent stake in the company, they are entitled to receive 20 per cent of Rs 12.6 crore, i.e. Rs 2.52 crore.

So finally, the investors receive a total of (2.4+2.52) crore, or Rs 4.92 crore.

It's easy to see how this arrangement is lopsided in favour of such investors. While they had only a 20 per cent stake, they ended up taking over 32 per cent of the final acquisition value owing to the liquidity preference and the participating nature of CCPS.

Example 2: 10 per cent CCPS at 2x participating liquidity preference

In this same example, if the investors had a 2x liquidity preference, they would be first entitled to 2x their principal + dividends, i.e. Rs 4.8 crore. Then, they would also claim 20 per cent of the Rs 10.2 crore surplus remaining, i.e. Rs 2.04 crore, finally earning Rs 6.84 crore.

It's clear that with investors having CCPS with participating liquidity preference greater than 1x, equity shareholders stand to gain substantially only when they're able to generate multifold returns. The larger the valuation, the smaller the significance of liquidity preference.

Example 3: 0.01 per cent CCPS at 1x non-participating liquidity preference

A non-participating liquidity preference bars the preference shareholders from claiming both their liquidation preference as well as participating in the surplus profits. They can either walk away with the principal + dividend or convert their preference shares to equity shares and obtain the same benefits as other equity shareholders.

Continuing with the same example where the investor put in Rs 2 crore for a 20 per cent stake, if they had 1x non-participating liquidation preference, they wouldn't get a share of the surplus left after receiving their principal and dividends. In this case, at the end of two years, they have negligible dividend accumulated since the rate is only 0.01 per cent. If the acquisition happens at Rs 15 crore and the investor chooses to convert the preference shares to equity shares, they simply get 20 per cent of the acquisition value, i.e. Rs 3 crore.

Alternatively, if they chose to not convert to equity shares, they would have the option to exit with their principal of Rs 2 crore and Rs 4000 accumulated as dividends. The 'non-participating' clause ensures only one of the two can be exercised.

In such cases, where investors have non-participating liquidity preference, they can choose to not convert their preference shares to equity if the acquisition happens at a valuation lower than what they invested at. Converting to equity would result in a loss on the principal invested. Holding and exercising their preference shares protects them from such a loss.

However, when the valuation is greater than when they invested, they can convert to equity and enjoy the upside along with other equity shareholders.

I advise founders to always negotiate for a 1x non-participating liquidity preference when issuing CCPS. As we saw in the examples above, a participating liquidity preference is heavily partial towards investors and leaves the founders with relatively little if the start-up doesn't do well. If the start-up does well, even with a non-participating liquidity preference, the investors anyway get their rightful claim to the upside.

CCPS with 1x non-participating liquidity preference is gradually becoming a standard because of its fairness to all stakeholders. But remember that an investor's lawyers may not set terms this way, so use this 'standard' as an anchor to negotiate. There can be scenarios built around liquidity preference that protect every party's interest fairly.

Also, at times, investors may prefer Optionally Convertible Redeemable Preference Shares (OCRPS) if they're not fully confident of the founders' ability or willingness to raise further rounds of funding.

For investors, an optionally convertible instrument like OCRPS helps their right to redeem their principal and seek it back at any time. They usually set predefined milestones on the achievement of which these options convert to shares. Again, this instrument too weighs heavily in the interest of investors, and I usually discourage founders from accepting any terms that are fraught with uncertainty.

c. Compulsorily Convertible Debentures

A compulsorily convertible debenture (CCD) is a bond that must convert to preference or equity shares on maturity. They typically start off and act as debt with a regular servicing of interest to the holders before converting to shares on the maturity date.

The paperwork for obtaining CCD is similar in length to CCPS. There is no minimum limit for investment by an investor through CCDs or CCPS. However, in CNs, each investor should invest a minimum of Rs 25 lakh as per current Indian corporate laws.

* * *

There are some more fundraising options available to founders, namely venture debt, revenue-based financing and community stock options (CSOPs). We have already discussed the concept of venture debt earlier in the book. Just to recap, venture debt firms offer unsecured loans at a relatively higher rate of interest while favouring start-ups that have found their product-market fit and have earned or raised enough capital to repay their debt in case things go south.

Let us delve into the concepts of revenue-based financing and that of CSOPs in some detail.

Revenue-Based Financing

This method of financing is eminently suitable for business models that are inherently scalable and do not need a constant influx of capital. Think SaaS products that need initial capital for product development and acquiring early users. Thereafter, revenues from operations may be enough to manage operational expenses. For such founders, raising money through equity financing may not be ideal. Revenue-based financing works far better for them, where investors get a percentage of future revenues in return for the money invested and there is no need for the founder to part with equity of the company. In turn, the founder can use the investment to enable greater sales and repay the investment from the revenues generated. Typically, this financing option is available to companies that are unit economics profitable and have consistent revenues. Besides SaaS products, D2C companies also often benefit from this financing method.

Here is a quick summary of some of the advantages that founders reap by way of revenue-based financing as opposed to raising venture capital or seeking a bank loan, for instance:

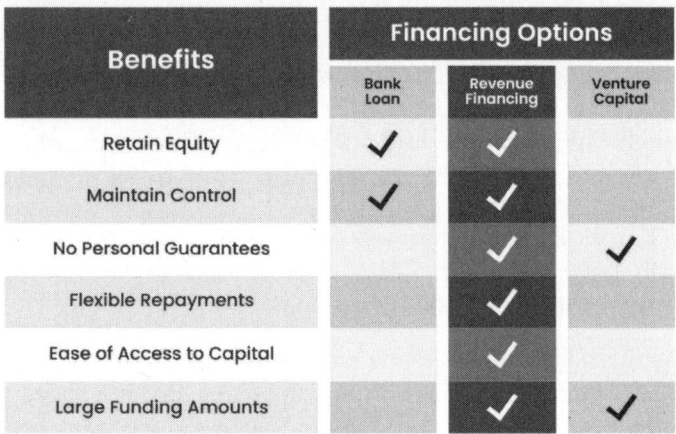

There are several investment firms that finance start-ups on a revenue basis, notable among them being Efficient Capital Labs, Klub, Getvantage, Velocity, Credavenue, n+1 Capital and Blacksoil. Most of these are registered as NBFCs. Many of them offer several different methods of financing, revenue financing being one of them. Sample the various financing options offered by Oxyzo, for instance:

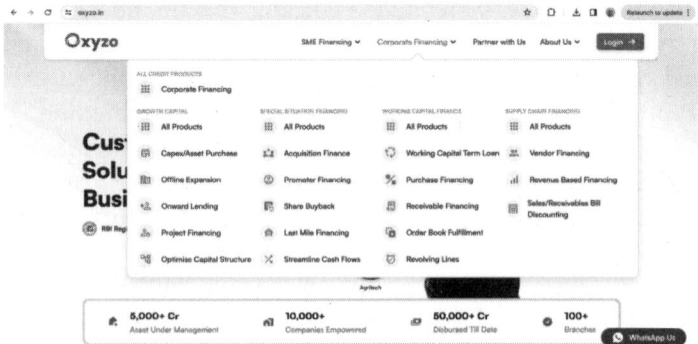

Community Stock Options

Some of you may recall an advertisement titled '*Main bhi angel*' that played during episodes of *Shark Tank*. The popularity of investing in start-ups was soaring at this point and the advert invited retail investors to be a part of the start-up ecosystem.

Think of it like equity-based crowdfunding, only that is not legally permissible in India. This was a workaround, bypassing traditional crowdfunding regulations. The move was positioned as one that would significantly broad-base private equity investing.

To begin with, let us understand the instrument used in this case—community stock options (CSOPs)—and how they are different from equity investment. CSOPs are a relatively new concept, often used by start-ups to raise funds while engaging their community of supporters. Unlike traditional stock options, CSOPs don't grant actual equity or voting rights in the company and do not put retail investors on the start-up's cap table. CSOPs often frame the participants as 'evangelists' or 'community members' rather than investors, which distinguishes them from traditional equity investments. Instead, they may offer benefits like stock appreciation rights (SARs), which allow holders to gain value if the company's market value increases, or perks like discounts on the company's products or services. These plans are designed to attract smaller investors who want to support start-ups without requiring large capital commitments.

Various platforms in India like Tyke Invest and Sateeq (which has now ceased operations), allow public investors to invest in various private limited companies vide this unique investment instrument. Let us see how the model works. As a start-up, you can approach one of these companies, who will then go on to set up a project on their website that allows retail investors to invest as low as Rs 5000 in the start-up. For the services, the platform charges a standard listing fee from the start-up and a success fee on the total amount raised.

While CSOPs were being positioned as ushering in a new era of start-up investment opportunities, they come with a host of issues. Importantly, CSOPs carry risks, such as limited regulatory oversight and the potential for companies to inflate revenues or delay buybacks of SARs. There have been instances of start-ups failing to deliver on promises made during fundraising campaigns. There have also been cases of regulatory violations that have raised concerns about the legitimacy of the instrument.

In an instance of Gurugram-based Solargridx Ventures Private Limited, which used the CSOP campaign on the Tyke platform under the brand name SustVest to raise around ~Rs 52 lakh from more than 500 investors, the Ministry of Corporate Affairs (MCA) issued an order against the company, imposing a total penalty of Rs 10 lakh on the company and the three directors for breach of section 42 of the Companies Act, 2013 (CA 2013). The MCA also asked the company to refund the total money received of ~Rs 52 lakh along with interest of ~Rs 7 lakh to the investors.[*]

While the company submitted that CSOPs are merely an agreement by the company to engage its subscribers/evangelists through a closed community with a view to grow the customer base and business, as per the MCA, however, CSOP is a 'derivative' as it derives its value from equity shares and thus should be treated as a 'security' requiring the company to comply with the provisions of section 42 of the CA 2013.

---

[*] Source: https://www.mca.gov.in/bin/dms/getdocument?mds=sBM4V De93G9p85DWpercent252BDkfvApercent253Dper cent253D&type=open.

Several start-up founders have reached out to me seeking advice on whether they should go ahead with CSOPs primarily as a means of bridge financing before they can lock in their next funding round. My advice to them has been to stay wary of such short-term capital options. While CSOPs can seem like an innovative option, start-ups must carefully evaluate the legal implications. I would much rather that start-ups go with the more traditional equity or the debt financing route. Additionally, for non-dilutive funding, they can also leverage schemes such as the Start-up Indian Seed Fund Scheme, an initiative by the Government of India to support early-stage start-ups.

Fundraising Paperwork and Compliance

Let us get now to the final segment, namely an overview of the paperwork you need to complete outside the term sheet to complete the fundraising process.

Definitive Agreements

By definition, a definitive agreement is a legally binding contract that finalizes the terms of a deal. In the context of start-up funding there are three definitive agreements that one must be aware of:

1. Share Purchase Agreement (SPA)
2. Share Subscription Agreement (SSA)
3. Shareholder's agreement (SHA)

During the early stages of a start-up, in the first or second round of investments, the SSA and the SHA are combined into one and called the share subscription and shareholder's agreement (SSHA).

Let us understand each of them in some detail.

Share Purchase Agreement

As its name suggests, a share purchase agreement (SPA) is necessitated when an individual or organization purchases the existing shares of the company from the founders or a shareholder. An SPA is necessary, for instance, when a VC firm purchases the shares of existing investors or when a start-up is being acquired. Essentially, this agreement details the share purchase transaction.

It typically includes details of:

1. **Parties Involved**: Identifies the buyer and seller, as well as the company whose shares are being sold.
2. **Shares and Purchase Price**: Specifies the number of shares being sold and the agreed-upon price.
3. **Representations and Warranties**: Includes assurances from both parties about the accuracy of information provided, such as the financial health of the company or the legal ownership of shares.
4. **Conditions Precedent**: Lists any conditions that must be met before the transaction can be completed, such as regulatory approvals or due diligence.
5. **Indemnities**: Protects the buyer or seller from specific risks or liabilities that may arise after the transaction.
6. **Governing Law**: States the legal jurisdiction under which the agreement will be enforced.

SPAs are designed to ensure transparency and protect the interests of both parties during the transaction.

Share Subscription Agreement

A **share subscription agreement (SSA)** is a legal contract between a company and an investor, where the investor agrees to subscribe to (i.e., purchase) newly issued shares of the company at an agreed-upon price. This agreement is commonly used by companies to raise capital, especially during early-stage funding or private placements.

Key features of a share subscription agreement include:

1. **Parties Involved**: The company issuing the shares and the investor subscribing to them.
2. **Number of Shares and Price**: Specifies the quantity of shares being issued and the price per share.
3. **Conditions Precedent**: Lists any conditions that must be fulfilled before the agreement becomes effective, such as regulatory approvals or due diligence.
4. **Conditions Subsequent**: Any conditions that must be fulfilled after the agreement becomes effective, again linked to regulatory approvals, and items agreed to be completed as per pre-determined timelines during the due diligence.
5. **Representations and Warranties**: Includes assurances from both parties, such as the company's financial health or the investor's ability to pay.
6. **Payment Terms**: Details how and when the investor will pay for the shares.
7. **Confidentiality Clause**: Ensures that sensitive information shared during the process remains confidential.
8. **Governing Law**: Specifies the legal jurisdiction under which the agreement will be enforced.

Shareholders' Agreement

A **shareholders' agreement** (SHA) is a legal contract between the shareholders of a company that outlines their rights, responsibilities and obligations, as well as how the company will be managed. It serves to protect the interests of shareholders and establish clear rules for decision-making and dispute resolution. Here are some key elements typically included in a shareholders' agreement:

1. **Ownership and Share Distribution**: Specifies the number of shares held by each shareholder and their percentage ownership in the company.
2. **Rights and Obligations**: Defines the rights of shareholders, such as voting rights, dividend entitlements and access to company information.
3. **Management and Decision-Making**: Outlines how the company will be managed, including the appointment of directors, board meetings and decision-making processes.
4. **Transfer of Shares**: Sets rules for transferring shares, including restrictions to prevent unwanted third parties from acquiring shares.
5. **Dispute Resolution**: Provides mechanisms for resolving disputes between shareholders, such as mediation or arbitration.
6. **Protection for Minority Shareholders**: Includes provisions to safeguard the interests of shareholders with less than 50 per cent ownership.
7. **Exit Strategies**: Details what happens if a shareholder wants to leave the company, including buyback options or share disposal rules.

The Steps to Create an SHA Include:

1. Ensuring a valuation certificate. There are three different laws under which valuation certification may be required:
    a) **The Income Tax Act, 1961:** Under this act, a valuation certificate is required from a merchant

banker. However, if your start-up is registered on the Start-up India website, is less than ten years old, does not have annual revenue of over Rs 100 crore and you have filled a declaration in Form 2 with the Income Tax Department, you are exempted from taking this certificate.

b) **The Companies Act, 2013:** Under this act, a valuation certificate is required from a registered valuer.

c) **The Foreign Exchange Management Act, 1999:** In case of a foreign investor, you need to take a valuation certificate from a registered valuer or chartered accountant, specifically stating that such certificate is for compliance with the Foreign Exchange Management Act (FEMA) guidelines. You also need to fill form FC-GPR with the RBI.

As these requirements are subject to change annually, I would strongly recommend you consult a lawyer and a tax adviser who are experienced in carrying out such transactions.

2. Define the number and category of shares allotted to investors.
3. Amend the Memorandum of Association to change the value of authorized capital and account for the new shares allotted to investors.
4. File the resolution with the Registrar of Companies (ROC) on the website of the Ministry of Corporate Affairs (MCA) in form MGT-14 as well as form SH7.
5. Convert the term sheet to a shareholders' agreement.
6. Call for an extraordinary general meeting of all shareholders to pass a resolution to approve the finalized agreements.
7. Incorporate the terms of the SHA into the Articles of Association (AoA) and approve them at a board meeting.

8. Copies of the amended AoA should be filed in form MGT-14 on the website of the MCA.
9. Open a separate bank account.
10. Carry out the allotment of shares in a board meeting.
11. Once shares are allotted to investors, form PAS-3 is filled with the MCA.
12. A written approval to PAS 3 and the last filled MGT-14 is received from the MCA.
13. Issue share certificates to all investors.
14. Get the share certificates signed from the local stamp duty office.

Getting through all of this, at first glance, does sound like a laborious task. As a knee-jerk reaction, start-up founders would rather let the investors take care of the definite agreements. However, there is merit in getting these agreements prepared yourself as you can anchor it in your needs while the negotiations, if any, are initiated by the other party.

Pro tip: In case the VCs insist on having the drafts prepared, be sure to negotiate a cap on lawyer's fees so you do not land up burning a hole in your pocket. Also, even if the drafts are being prepared by the VC, do ensure you have a legal consultant who can study the documents on your behalf.

As for the transaction costs involved in drafting a shareholder's agreement, it varies with the funding round, size of investment, investment instruments, etc. When you are raising money in the form of a convertible note, for instance, the professional charges and lawyer's fees may amount to Rs 50,000. However, if an investment of Rs 2–3 crore occurs in a valued round in the form of CCPS or CCDs, the cost may approximate Rs 2–3 lakh. When a marquee investor comes on board, the fee could be considerably higher and a fee cap is best discussed.

As a thumb rule you can expect the total cost of fundraising to be around 4 per cent of the transaction size, especially if an investment banker is also involved.

Section Seven

Basics of Business Compliance That a Founder Must Know

- Types of Business Entities—Set-up, Costs, Compliance
- Goods and Services Tax
- TDS and TCS

While we have looked at several strategic aspects of setting up a business through the various sections of this book, before we close, it will be worthwhile to spend some time discussing some basics of compliance that every founder must be aware of. As they say, knowledge is power. It is best therefore to be prepared well and avoid any unnecessary troubles.

Types of Business Entities—Set-up, Costs, Compliance

Let us begin the compliance discussion with the very basics: the types of business entities that you can set up.

It has been my experience that having found an idea and willing partners, entrepreneurs often rush to register a company without spending much time on evaluating the pros and cons of different types of business entities. Much as incorporating a company gives the founders a great high on achieving an important milestone, the decision must take into account several aspects, including the not-so-fortunate eventuality of having to shut down your start-up in future. In such a situation, you shouldn't be dragged into a compliance quicksand. For erstwhile entrepreneurs, struggling to shut down businesses and spending money on an entity with non-existent revenues isn't the most desirable outcome.

The subsequent sections cover the business entities of a proprietorship, partnership, LLP, OPC, and private limited company. We will discuss the basic characteristics of the entity, who should consider registering it, the process of registration and shutting down, and a comparison of pros and cons for each of them. Following that, we talk about the different countries where you may register your start-up.

In the event that you haven't registered your entity yet, I'd urge you to go through the discussion carefully to make an informed decision. Feel free to skip this section, if you have already registered a business entity.

What Kind of Company to Register?

Founders are intuitively inclined to register a Private Limited Company because that is believed to be most visible. However, many would be better off registering a different entity depending on the type of business and the stage they are in. Let us understand the options available in India.

Proprietorship

Proprietorship works best if you are a solopreneur or work in a small team, and have a predominantly service-based model. Freelancers of all types can operate as sole proprietors under a business name to lend themselves more credibility. Essentially, it's the founder operating with just a business name officially allotted.

It must be noted that a proprietorship brings unlimited liability to the founders. It means that anything attributed to the business—complaints, financial irregularities, etc.—makes the founder directly responsible for it. Unlike a private limited company, proprietorship is not considered an entity separate from the founder. Some proprietors take professional indemnity insurance to mitigate the risk. It is a scheme that protects one from professional negligence or cases where you can be sued by your client for unsatisfactory service. The insurance covers the cost. But it has its limitations concerning the total coverage, so any such insurance scheme must be thoroughly inspected before signing up.

Overall, proprietorship is a great means to start a business officially for its ease of compliance and even shutting down. It also allows complete secrecy of the business financials, which is not the case with a private limited company. Even taxes are paid as per your individual income slab, whereas in a private limited company, a flat 30 per cent of profits is paid as taxes.

Registration

- No separate registration is required to work as a proprietorship. You may require a GST Identification Number (GSTIN) if revenues cross the threshold, such as Rs 20 lakh in sales in a year, or you wish to engage in inter-state sales in India.

- You may have to open a current account with any bank with your personal details and ID proofs. This accounts for the business receipts, savings for salary incomes, etc.
- For the tradename, you have to file a UDYAM registration under the MSME Act. The process of this registration is easy and can be completed online within a few minutes.
- You may also require a Shop and Establishment registration and a CA certificate of the ownership of the tradename. The registration of a proprietorship generally costs less than Rs 5000. This cost (and the ones mentioned for the other entities) is exclusive of the income tax and GST compliances.

Shutting Down

To shut down a proprietorship, there's barely any cost. You just need to close the bank account, surrender the GSTIN and file the business income and expense details in your personal income tax return (ITR).

Partnership

A partnership, very simply put, is a proprietorship but with multiple business partners. A simple agreement is done between the business owners or partners on all the different terms of business—functional responsibilities, decision-making powers, profit split, salaries, etc.

All other functional parameters, benefits and disadvantages are almost the same as in a proprietorship.

Registration

- The partners mention the terms on which they plan to run the business in a partnership deed and print it on

stamp paper. The stamp duty varies from state to state and on the capital contribution of the partners.
- After the partnership deed is printed, they apply for a permanent account number (PAN).
- Once they receive their PAN, they can open a bank account and commence business activities.

A partnership may also need a Shop and Establishment Registration and GSTIN to open a bank account. The registration of a partnership generally costs around Rs 5000–Rs 10,000. The Indian Partnership Act defines two different types of partnerships:

Registered Partnership	Unregistered Partnership
The partnership deed is registered at the local registrar of the firm's office in the appropriate jurisdiction.	No such registration.
Can sue a third party as it is a registered entity in the eyes of the law.	In this case, only the partners can sue each other but not any third party because the contract is only between them.

Shutting Down

To shut down a partnership, the founders need to file their ITR, surrender the GSTIN and make a dissolution deed by which they distribute assets and liabilities between themselves.

There's a minimal cost of doing the paperwork of dissolving a partnership and it takes about two months. The process is much easier if the necessary agreements have been done between the partners.

Limited Liability Partnership (LLP)

LLP as an entity was introduced in the Limited Liability Partnership Act of 2008. The objective was to solve the problem of unlimited liability that came with a proprietorship or partnership. While a private limited company was still an option for such businesses, the delta between this and a partnership was huge in terms of compliances and ease of setting up and shutting down. Moreover, such businesses didn't need many of the key provisions offered by a private limited company, such as raising external funds or granting ESOPs to their employees. The issue was mainly of unlimited liability, which could potentially create unnecessary problems for the founders, especially after the business grew and comprised different moving parts.

LLP was introduced mainly to enable multiple partners belonging to the same profession to set up an entity with limited liability. A team of lawyers, for example, could come together and start a legal consultancy business under an LLP.

Similarly, a group of architects could join hands and start an architecture firm. The nature of these professions is such that if something goes wrong, an unlimited liability on the personal assets of a partner can be unjustifiably high. For example, if an architect designs a house for an individual, and later after its construction, some faults are discovered, it may not necessarily have been the architect's wrongdoing.

In such a case, if the individual sues the architect, there's an unnecessary liability on them personally.

LLPs were incepted mainly to give limited liability to a partnership, to avoid cases like the one mentioned above. A private limited company could also have been an option, but such firms don't need external funding or need to give away ESOPs, and they don't intend to lose the secrecy of their financials, so it would have been unnecessary.

In an LLP, if two partners have invested Rs 1 lakh each, and the company makes a profit of Rs 3 lakh over time, the total capital of the LLP amounts to Rs 5 lakh. If anyone sues the LLP, the liability will be limited to the value of the asset or money, which is Rs 5 lakh in this example. Any legal case or suit for recovery beyond this amount will be invalid as the LLP does not have that much money. So the partners are insulated from the risk of having to liquidate their personal assets to pay for damages.

LLP thus provides a good middle ground between a partnership and a private limited company.

Registration

- A partnership deed, containing the terms of execution of the business, is printed on a stamp paper and signed by all the partners.
- The LLP then needs to be registered on the MCA portal with the MCA.
- The name of the LLP needs to be approved by the MCA. The name needs to be representative of the industry the LLP will function in and will have the suffix 'LLP'.
- An LLP also has certain filing requirements. If the capital contribution in the partnership is more than Rs 25 lakh or the total turnover of the business for a year is more than Rs 40 lakh, then a statutory audit by a CA on an annual basis is mandatory.
- An LLP has to ensure a mandatory annual filing with the MCA, in addition to ITR filing and GST filing.
- The directors' KYC needs to be done online on the MCA portal every year. The registration of an LLP generally costs around Rs 7500–15,000.

Shutting down

Shutting down an LLP requires more effort in executing the paperwork and filing it on the MCA portal compared to a partnership, but easier than a private limited company.

It can only be shut with all filings done and approval obtained from the MCA, which can take about six to twelve months to complete.

Private Limited

'Private Limited' (Pvt. Ltd) allows a business to run as a full-fledged business entity with no liability to the founders, permits it to raise external funds and grant ESOPs to employees, and gives it a professional look. If you plan to build a company with multiple stakeholders in the business, it's best to register as a Pvt. Ltd under the Companies Act 2013.

Registration

Every Pvt. Ltd entity needs to have a Memorandum of Association (MoA), Articles of Association (AoA) and Certificate of Incorporation (CoI).

- The first step in the registration is the name approval.
- A Pvt. Ltd entity needs to have a minimum of two shareholders and directors. Solo founders often enlist a family member as the second shareholder and director.
- A Pvt. Ltd is required to have at least four board meetings in a financial year and the difference between two board meetings cannot be more than 120 days. At least one director of the company has to be in India for more than 182 days in a year.
- An annual audit by a CA is mandatory for a Pvt. Ltd. The financial statements, balance sheet, P&L statement, audit report, etc., have to be filed on the MCA portal. Moreover, these documents are publicly available at a nominal price.

The registration of a Pvt. Ltd generally costs less than Rs 15,000–Rs 30,000. It can vary based on the amount of initial capital invested, and the number of directors and shareholders.

Shutting Down

- Shutting down a Pvt. Ltd is the most arduous among all entities.
- You can shut down a Pvt. Ltd only after approval from the MCA or Registrar of Companies (RoC).
- You need to get a 'No Objection' certificate from the GST department, the Income Tax department and other relevant departments to ensure that the entity does not have any external liabilities.
- The directors and shareholders need to give indemnities to the government so that if any liability arises in the future, the directors will be personally liable for it.
- There has to be no business for a minimum period of two years if you have run the business for a couple of years or more.

Certain schemes are offered from time to time that expedite the process of shutting down. But if no such scheme is in place, then the process is time-consuming. It costs at least Rs 20,000 to shut one down, and can take one or two years or even more.

One Person Company

The One Person Company (OPC) was introduced as a concept in the Companies Act 2013 to help plug some gaps that a Pvt. Ltd or an LLP alone couldn't provide. For example, if a single person wanted to register a Pvt. Ltd, they needed to bring along another shareholder and director just to show it on paper, as it was mandatory to have two directors as well as shareholders. This created obstacles and unnecessary liability for the silent director and shareholder.

OPC removed these hurdles and allowed a single person to be named director, with just a nominee added in case the director expired during the tenure. The name of the company should mandatorily end with '(OPC) Pvt. Ltd'. Earlier, the OPC provision was capped at Rs 2 crore annual revenue, after which it had to mandatorily convert to a Pvt. Ltd, but now the limits have been removed.

However, an OPC can't raise external funds, give ESOPs or have any other shareholders. They would need to be converted into a Pvt. Ltd to enable these.

So, OPC is great for a solo founder who wants to register their business professionally but maintain limited liability. In other words, it's a more secure form of proprietorship for them.

Registration

The registration takes place with the MCA and there is only one person who acts as the shareholder and the director. The process otherwise is similar to a Pvt. Ltd.

Shutting Down

The process, again, is similar to a private limited company, but can be slightly easier since there's just one shareholder and director, which reduces the compliance needs.

The following table can be referred to for a good summary of all these entities.

Entity	Who should consider	Pros	Cons
Proprietorship	Solopreneur/Freelancer	–Low registration cost –Ease of registering –Ease of shutting down –Potentially lower taxes	–Unlimited liability –Can't accept external equity funds –Can't offer ESOPs –Can't have official business partners
Partnership	Two or more co-founders building a service business or just testing the waters before a larger foray	–Can have multiple co-founders –Low cost of registration –Relative ease of registering and shutting down	–Unlimited liability on founders –Can't accept external funds –Can't offer ESOPs
Limited Liability Partnership (LLP)	Group of professionals providing a service prone to liability—doctors, lawyers, architects, CAs, etc.	–Liability to partners limited to the total value of assets in LLP –Low cost of registration –Gives a more professional outlook than proprietorship or partnership—can be converted to Pvt. Ltd any time	–Higher cost of maintenance than Proprietorship/Partnership—Can't accept external equity funds—Can't offer ESOPs

Entity	Who should consider	Pros	Cons
Private Limited (Pvt. Ltd)	Anyone looking to build a large company and have multiple shareholders in the form of investors and employees	–Liability to founders is limited –Allows external funding –Easy transferability of shares –Different categories of shareholders can be created –Succession planning is easiest	–Highest maintenance cost –Shutting down can take painfully long and cost the most –Company financials can be accessed by competitors
One Person Company (OPC)	Solo founder seeking limited liability	–Protection against unlimited liability –No requirement of a silent director or shareholder	–Can't accept external equity funds –Long-drawn-out shutting down process

Afterword

As we reach the end of this journey, I want to take a moment to reflect on the inspiration behind writing this book and, of course, acknowledge the many contributors who have made this book possible.

This book is dedicated to the vibrant and dynamic landscape of the Indian entrepreneurial experience—a realm filled with immense potential and a wealth of opportunity. The entrepreneurial spirit in India is not merely about starting businesses; it's an intricate dance of innovation, resilience and community-building. My hope is that this book serves as a guiding light for those who dare to follow this path.

Throughout my journey, I have had the privilege of standing on the shoulders of giants—mentors and industry leaders who have generously shared their knowledge and experiences with me. Their insights and contributions have profoundly shaped the perspectives shared here. I have also been lucky that my experiences as an adviser to various start-ups, across domains, has offered me a front-row seat to the triumphs and challenges faced by entrepreneurs. This book draws on the diverse experiences and knowledge of many individuals who have generously shared their insights and expertise, in creating what I hope is a rich tapestry of learning for readers.

While this book does not claim to cover every conceivable aspect of building a start-up, I have made a concerted effort to address the most vital components that aspiring founders encounter—from generating innovative business ideas to navigating the intricacies of raising funds and understanding compliance essentials. As far as possible, I have also tried to infuse each chapter with practical advice designed to empower entrepreneurs, helping them turn their vision into reality.

In closing, I would like to acknowledge several people who have supported me throughout this endeavour.

Acknowledgements

First and foremost, to my parents—your guidance, both personal and professional, has shaped me into the person I am today. Every lesson, every conversation, every moment of support over the years has contributed to this journey. As a firm believer in the butterfly effect, I wouldn't change a single thing about the path that led me here.

To my wife, Aditi, who wears many hats in my life with remarkable grace. As my business partner in our investment banking practice, you've been my greatest teacher in the art of pitching, sales and branding—skills that form the very foundation of this book. On a personal level, you're my strongest advocate, always ensuring I put my best foot forward. Your unwavering belief in me has been the wind beneath my wings throughout this entire process.

To the exceptional team at Penguin Random House India, particularly Rinku Paul and Radhika Marwah—thank you for believing in this project and helping me find my authentic voice on these pages. Your editorial expertise and collaborative spirit have been instrumental in bringing *The Money Ball* to life in its truest essence.

Finally, to every entrepreneur who has ever dared to dream, pitch and persevere—this book is for you. May your ideas find the capital they deserve, and may your ventures change the world.

I have compiled a list of investors, templates of legal documentation used at the time of fundraising, and checklists that could be helpful to you as a founder. You can access them by scanning the QR code below.

Scan QR code to access the
Penguin Random House India website